USELESS KNOWLEDGE

SPORTS

FEATS *and* DEFEATS

150 Answers to Questions You Never Thought to Ask

Publications International, Ltd.

Front cover images: Getty, Shutterstock.com

Back cover images: Getty

Interior images: All from Art Explosion except page 9, Jordan Kost; page 33, Clipart.com; page 95, Getty; page 137, Shutterstock.com

Contributing writers: Angelique Anacleto, Brett Ballantini, Diane Lanzillotta Bobis, Joshua D. Boeringa, Shelley Bueché, Michelle Burton, Steve Cameron, Matt Clark, Anthony G. Craine, Dan Dalton, Paul Forrester, Shanna Freeman, Chuck Giamatta, Ed Grabianowski, Jack Greer, Tom Harris, Vickey Kalambakal, Brett Kyle, Noah Liberman, Letty Livingston, Alex Nechas, Jessica Royer Ocken, Thad Plumley, ArLynn Leiber Presser, Pat Sherman, William Wagner, Carrie Williford

Louis Weber, CEO
Publications International, Ltd.
7373 North Cicero Avenue
Lincolnwood, Illinois 60712

Permission is never granted for commercial purposes.

ISBN: 978-1-4508-9335-0

Manufactured in U.S.A.

8 7 6 5 4 3 2 1

CONTENTS

Chapter 1: **Across Sports**   6

Including: How do bookies set odds on sporting events? • Which sport
has the greatest athletes? • Which sport has the worst athletes? •
Who are the most underpaid athletes? • What's the difference between
billiards and pool? • Why do most sports go counterclockwise?

Chapter 2: **Events to Remember**   38

Including: Which teams were involved in the football play known as "The
Immaculate Reception"? • Which team used a "College of Coaches"?
• What children's movie interrupted coverage of a 1968 Jets-Raiders
game? • What year did an earthquake interrupt the World Series?

Chapter 3: **Getting Into Gear**   56

Including: What is the uniform for underwater hockey? • How do corked
bats help cheating baseball players hit the ball farther? • Why is a
football shaped that way? • Why would you want to put "English" on the
cue ball? • Who invented the jockstrap?

Chapter 4: **Grab Bag**   78

Including: What stadium is referrred to as "The House That Doak Built"?
• What sports have been traditionally associated with Christmas in
America? • Was professional wrestling ever real? • How high can you
legally dribble a basketball? • Does a curveball really curve?

Chapter 5: **How and Why**   94

Including: Why isn't a boxing ring round? • Why do golfers hate to putt?
• Why is soccer popular everywhere except the United States? • Why do
the Dallas Cowboys and Detroit Lions always play on Thanksgiving? •
Why is a marathon 26.2 miles?

Chapter 6: **How It All Got Started**   123

Including: What were baseball's predecessors? • When was AstroTurf
invented? • Where did the trampoline come from? • How did modern
bowling develop? • Who wrote "Take Me Out to the Ball Game"? • How
did football become the game it is today?

Chapter 7: **Language and Lingo**   152

Including: When did fans from Wisconsin first call themselves
Cheeseheads? • What sport's name means "the bishop's staff"? • How
did the Super Bowl gets its name? • Why is the St. Louis baseball team
called the Cardinals, even though Missouri's state bird is the bluebird?

Chapter 8: **Myths and Truths**   181

Including: Did Leo Durocher really coin the phrase "nice guys finish
last"? • Is the Heisman Trophy cursed? • Can a sports game have an
effect on a city's sewage system? • Is the gambling industry rigged in
favor of the house?

Chapter 9: **The Olympic Games** 192

Including: What were the ancient Olympic Games like? • Who was the first Olympic champion in the modern games? • In the 1936 Olympics, which American won the gold medal in the 800-meter race? • Does buzkashi have any chance of becoming an Olympic sport?

Chapter 10: **Feats and Facts for the History Books** 208

Including: Which hockey player has spent the most time in the penalty box? • What popular sporting events of the early 1900s lasted six days? • Who was the worst team in major league baseball history? • Which baseball card is worth the most?

Chapter 11: **Remarkable People** 229

Including: Who was the first African American player in the American League? • Which great female athlete once struck out Joe DiMaggio? • Who was the first and only heavyweight champion to retire undefeated? • Who was Simonya Popova?

Chapter 12: **The Odd, the Obscure, and the Just Plain Strange** 258

Including: What happens when animals get on the baseball field? • Where do toe wrestlers complete? • What do the winners in a cheese-rolling contest bring home?

Chapter 1
ACROSS SPORTS

Q How do bookies set odds on sporting events?

A To answer this question, we need to learn a little about the sports book biz. Consider this gambling primer: Bookies take a small percentage of every bet that comes in; this is known as the vig. The ideal situation for any bookie is to have an equal amount of money riding on both sides of a bet; this way, no matter what happens in the game, the bookie will make money. The bookie will pay out money to those who bet on the winner, take in money from those who bet on the loser, and come out ahead because of the vig.

If everyone bets on one team and that team wins, the bookie will lose a lot of money. Sports odds are designed to keep an even number of bettors on each side of the bet.

Major sports books in Las Vegas and Europe employ experienced oddsmakers to set the point spread, odds, or money line on a game. Oddsmakers must know a lot about sports and a lot about gamblers: They examine every detail of an upcoming game—including public perceptions about it—to determine which team has the better chance of winning. Several days or weeks prior to the game, the oddsmakers meet, compare information, and reach a consensus on the odds.

Here's a simple example: Team A is thought to be much better than Team B in an upcoming game. If both sides of the bet paid off the same amount of money, almost everyone would bet on Team A. The oddsmakers try to determine what odds will even out the betting. Giving Team B five-to-one odds means anyone who bets on Team B will make five times his bet if Team B wins. Team B may not have much of a chance of winning, but the increased reward makes the risk worthwhile to gamblers.

Or, depending on the sport and the country, the oddsmakers might set a money line, which is usually expressed as a "plus" or "minus" dollar amount. This is effectively the same thing as setting odds—the money line simply reflects the payoff that a bettor can expect from a winning bet.

Another way to balance the betting market is with a point spread. In this case, winning bets always pay off at one-to-one, or even odds, usually with a ten percent vig on top, which means you would have to bet eleven dollars to win ten dollars. The point spread handicaps the game in favor of one team. In, say, football, Team A might get a spread of minus-seven. This means gamblers aren't just betting on whether Team A will win, but on whether it will do so by more than seven points.

Odds can change leading up to an event. This might indicate something significant happened, such as an injury to a key player, or it might mean that bookies are adjusting the odds because too many bets were coming in on one side. Adjusting the odds reflects their attempt to balance the betting and minimize their potential loss. Remember, a bookie isn't in this for fun and games—he's in it to make profits. And at the end of the day, he's the one who almost always wins.

What are the differences between Canadian and American football?

 Football, no matter where it's played, is derived from an impromptu sport developed at Rugby School in England back in 1823 and credited to William Webb Ellis. Today, it's played in different countries under varying rules. Here are some of the changes between the sport as it's played in the United States and its neighbor to the north.

The American football field is 100 yards long and 53 1/3 yards wide. The Canadian field is larger—110 yards long and 65 yards wide.

Canadian football places the goalposts on the goal line. American football places them behind the end zone.

American teams are allowed eleven players on the field at one time. Canadian teams can use twelve.

On kickoff, American receivers can call a fair catch, downing the ball when they catch it. Canada has no such rule, but the kicking team must give the player catching the ball a five-yard buffer zone.

Canadian players have to move more quickly between plays, having only twenty seconds on the play clock from the end of one play to when the ball is snapped for the next. American players have a luxurious forty seconds to run a new play after the ball was downed on the previous one; if the clock was stopped between plays, they have twenty-five seconds from when it is restarted.

American teams get a two-minute warning before the end of a half. The Canadian warning is three minutes.

When lining up for a play, all offensive players in the Canadian backfield (except the quarterback) are allowed to be in motion. In American football, not so much—only one player can be in motion.

American teams at the line of scrimmage are separated by only the length of the football. Canadian teams must line up a yard apart.

If a Canadian team misses a field goal, the defensive team can run it out of the end zone; if the defense fails to do so, the kick is worth a point. When an American team muffs a field goal outside the 20-yard line, its opponent gets a first down at the same line of scrimmage.

And if you think Canadian football is different, you'd be shocked by the Australian version, where the football field (or pitch, as it's called) is an oval rather than the familiar rectangle, there are 18 players from each team on the field at any given time, and none wear any protective equipment—the uniform consists of shorts, sleeveless shirts, and studded boats (shoes). Not only that, but players may either run with a ball or kick it, but they cannot pass it. If a player chooses to run with the ball, it must be bounced on the ground once every fifteen meters (about fifty feet).

What sports did people play in Biblical times?

 Today, some famous athletes pray to or thank Jesus for their victories. But with what sports would Jesus himself have been familiar?

In 1 Corinthians 9:24–27, Paul speaks of physical training and running races. The people of the Bible were very much like us, and they enjoyed the competition and fellowship of participating in contests that challenged them physically and mentally. Some biblical archaeological studies refer to ancient sports and recreation. These included primitive versions of soccer, cricket, field hockey, and a baseball-like game called round ball.

The Bible doesn't list specific games that children played, but in Zechariah 8:5 it mentions, "boys and girls playing in [Jerusalem's] streets." And in Matthew 11:16–17, Jesus speaks of children singing songs to each other. Most of their games were probably played out-doors, such as running races, participating in feats of strength and agility, and using slingshots. Bible-time children played ball games with a ball probably made of solid leather. Girls played knuckle-bones, which is like jacks. Archaeologists have found marked-off squares that could have been used for hopscotch. Rattles, whistles, game boards, tiny clay pots, marbles, and furniture have also been found in some digs.

Which sport has the greatest athletes?

 Sometimes the simplest questions are the most complicated to answer. Even if you agree on the criteria for which sport has the greatest athletes—strength, agility, endurance, coordination, all of the above, or some of the above—you come up with no consensus on the answer. So let's start by running down some of the experts' opinions.

Canada's Sun Media newspapers published a series of articles in 2007 in which five sports were analyzed—basketball, baseball, football, hockey, and soccer—and the arguments for soccer players being the greatest athletes seemed the most persuasive. Soccer players run six miles or more per game, combining jogging and sprinting for ninety minutes. There are changes of direction, vertical jumps, astounding acts of agility, one-on-one battles that often get physical, and the need to be just as sharp in the ninetieth minute as in the first. The writer called soccer the most physically demanding team sport.

However, Sun Media's own medical expert, Dr. Bob Litchfield, medical director of the Fowler Kennedy Sports Medicine Clinic at the University of Western Ontario, cast his vote for basketball because of the wear and tear players in that sport—particularly NBA guards—must endure.

When the scope is widened beyond major sports, other athletes make powerful cases. The *St. Petersburg Times* in Florida did research in 2004 and decided the toughest sport is—drum roll, please—water polo. Sorry, but there's something anticlimactic about that one.

For another perspective, the *Times* talked to Dr. Peter Davis, director of coaching and sports sciences for the United States Olympic Committee (USOC). Davis presumably has the kind of broad-based practical experience necessary to render an objective answer. "My vote for world's best athlete? I'd say an Australian Rules football player," Davis said. "Then again, I'm biased. I'm from Australia."

Davis noted that USOC scientists consider synchronized swimming the most grueling sport. "Try treading water for a minute while making perfectly choreographed movements. And, oh yeah, do it upside down, under water," he said.

Men's Journal magazine did its top ten in 2003 and decided on gymnastics, followed by the Ironman triathlon, rock climbing, hockey, bull riding, boxing, rugby, decathlon, water polo, and football. No soccer, basketball, Australian Rules football, endurance bicycling, or synchronized swimming. See how hard it is to find a consensus?

Then there are the oh-so-clever pundits who claim that racehorses are the best athletes. Yes, they're powerful, graceful, and fast. But have you ever seen a horse hit a curveball?

As you can see, the answer to this question is completely subjective. Our vote goes for basketball, which combines all of soccer's strength and agility needs with most of its endurance demands, then layers on the whole upper-body thing plus equal or greater degrees of physical contact. Then again, we could just throw up our hands and vote for poker players. After all, they have to worry about hemorrhoids. And those things are painful.

 Which sport has the worst athletes?

 We know what you're thinking: bowling. It's an obvious choice, but you're wrong. We know what you've seen at your local bowling alley, and, yes, it's tragic. But comparing those people to pro bowlers, who need the physical and mental stamina to compete on far less forgiving lanes and bowl up to one hundred games a week, is like comparing those chunky, redfaced softball players at your local park to major-league baseball players.

And no, it's not baseball, either—John Kruk notwithstanding. (In response to a fan who chided him during his playing days for his less-than-exemplary physique, the corpulent Kruk replied, "I ain't an athlete, lady, I'm a baseball player.")

Golf is a common target for those who wish to identify nonathletes, and the sport has indeed featured some Krukian figures, such as the generously proportioned John Daly. Still, the strength and stamina it takes to get that darned ball from the tee to the hole—while walking about twenty to twenty-five miles over the course of a tournament— qualifies as athletic prowess. (You snicker, but when was the last time you walked twenty-five miles in a week?)

How about the luge? Now we're getting somewhere. Who among us hasn't spent an entire Sunday afternoon "practicing the luge"(i.e., prostrate on the couch in front of the TV, watching other people sweat)? Turns out, though, that real lugers have tremendous upper-body strength and spend their off-seasons lifting weights and swim-ming. Who knew?

So we turn to curling, which, as we are all aware, is basically just shuffleboard for aging Canadians who haven't yet broken their hips. At the 2006 Winter Olympics, United States curler Scott Baird competed at the age of fifty-four. And yet, there is agility involved— it's kind of like bowling on ice. And did you see that "women of curling" nude calendar that made a splash during those same 2006

Olympics? We defy you to tell us that those bodies weren't athletic. So curling's out.

Okay, time to get serious. Which sport has the worst athletes? We planned to choose darts, which requires participants to spend as much time as possible in bars, where breaking a sweat has more to do with the TV lighting than the action. But then we stumbled upon the Cyberathlete Professional League (CPL). That's right: professional video gamers posing as athletes.

Sure, this seems like a typical case of the jocks picking on the nerds. But the CPL (before it folded in 2008) went to great lengths to portray itself as a real, big-time sports league, right down to its red, white, and blue logo that mimicked the classic NBA and Major League Baseball logos—a silhouetted figure (seated, of course) wearing headphones and pumping one fist in the air exultantly while the other hand daintily fingers a mouse. In other words, they were asking for it. A sport of computer geeks. A sport with an "official pizza" (Pizza Hut). That's the sport with the worst athletes.

Q Which sports burn the most calories?

A Everybody wants to burn the most calories in the least amount of time. Of course, how many calories you burn depends on how hard you work out and how much you weigh. Here are some popular activities that burn a lot of calories. (These estimates are based on a 150-pound person; a heavier person will burn more.)

Burning about 450 calories every 30 minutes (based on an 8-minute mile), running also gives a fantastic cardiorespiratory workout. Leg strength and endurance are maximized, but few benefits accrue to the upper body.

Rock climbing relies on quick bursts of energy to get from one rock to the next. It won't do a lot for your heart, but your strength, endurance, and flexibility will greatly benefit, and you'll burn about 371 calories every half hour.

Swimming provides an excellent overall body workout, burning up to 360 calories in a half hour depending on the stroke used. However, most people have difficulty maintaining proper form for that long. The best swim workout is based on interval training: swim two lengths, catch your breath, and then repeat.

Depending on your speed, cycling burns around 300 or 400 calories in a half hour. It provides a great cardio workout and builds up those thighs and calves.

If you're game enough to step into the boxing ring, you'll be rewarded with a 324-calorie deficit for every half hour of slugging it out. In addition, your cardiorespiratory fitness and muscular endurance will go through the roof. Make sure you're match fit, though, or it may be all over before you build up a sweat!

Churning through about 300 calories in 30 minutes, racquetball gives you a fantastic cardiorespiratory workout, builds lower body strength and endurance, and with all that twisting and pivoting, develops great flexibility around the core.

The nonstop action of basketball will see you dropping around 288 calories every half hour, while at the same time developing flexibility, endurance, and cardiorespiratory health. But warm up properly because the sudden twists and turns can be high risk for the unprepared.

Burning about 280 calories per half hour, rowing is a very effective way to rid yourself of extra energy. It also builds up endurance, strength, and muscle in your shoulders, thighs, and biceps. Kayaking and canoeing each burn around 170 calories in a half hour.

Tennis consumes about 250-300 calories in a half hour session, providing a great opportunity to burn excess calories while developing cardiorespiratory fitness.

With cross-country skiing, the very fact that you're out in the snow has already fired up your metabolism. As soon as you start mushing through it, you'll be churning through those calories at the rate of 270 every half hour.

Ice skating gives you all the benefits of running without the joint stress. A half hour on the ice consumes about 252 calories.

Yes, you can dance your way to fitness! Swing dancing burns about 180 calories in a half hour and gives you a moderately intense aerobic workout.

What are some of the strangest college mascots?

A College sports brim with colors, birds, wildcats, tigers, and bears in some form or other. Common pooches abound, from bulldogs to wolves. There are numerous ancient warriors, such as Spartans and Trojans. But for us, these are the mascots that deserve the highest marks for originality.

Banana Slugs (University of California–Santa Cruz): If a slug suggests a lethargic or reluctant team, that's just what students had in mind when they chose the image. The bright yellow banana slug lives amid the redwoods on campus and represents a mild protest of the highly competitive nature of most college sports.

Boll Weevils/Cotton Blossoms (University of Arkansas–Monticello, men/women): When cotton ruled Dixie, the boll weevil was more fearsome than any snake. Evidently, the women's teams didn't care to be named after an invasive insect, and who can blame them?

Crimson Tide (University of Alabama): The school's teams have always worn crimson, but the term "Crimson Tide" seems to have been popularized by sportswriters waxing poetic about epic struggles in mud and rain.

Eutectics (St. Louis College of Pharmacy, Missouri): The word "Eutectic" refers to the chemical process in which two solids become a liquid, representing the school's integration of competitive athletics and rigorous academic programs. ESPN recognized the Eutectic—a furry creature dressed in a lab coat—as one of the most esoteric mascots in the country.

Governors (Austin Peay, Tennessee): This one made sense, as the school is named for the Tennessee governor who signed the bill establishing it. At least "Governors" is more inspiring than the old nickname, "Normalities." One wonders how the eminent statesman would react to the popular student cheer today: "Let's go Peay!"

Ichabods (Washburn University, Kansas, men): An Ichabod would be, at the least, a generous man. Washburn University was established as Lincoln College, but it ran out of money. When philanthropist Ichabod Washburn bailed out Lincoln, the grateful school renamed itself. This may disappoint everyone who references the headless ghost in *The Legend of Sleepy Hollow*, but Washburn University's version is still a worthy tale. The women's teams are the Lady Blues.

Jennies (Central Missouri State, women): A jenny is a female donkey, but this name makes sense only when put in context: The school's men's teams are the Mules. Both are a big improvement on "Normals" and "Teachers," the names used before 1922.

Paladins (Furman University, South Carolina): A paladin is a pious, righteous knight. The title originally belonged to the 12 peers of Charlemagne's court.

Poets (Whittier College, California): If opponents don't exactly tremble when the Whittier mascot takes the field, it's because he's a big-headed figure who dresses in colonial garb and carries a pen and pad. The school was named for poet John Greenleaf Whittier.

Ragin' Cajuns (University of Louisiana–Lafayette): The name refers, of course, to the region's feisty Cajun ethnic heritage. Fans hold up signs saying "Geaux Cajuns!" Although decidedly not French, it certainly gets the message across.

Rainbow Wahine (University of Hawaii, women): Hawaii has an interesting situation because it chose to let its teams name themselves by sport. Some men's teams are the Warriors, some are the Rainbows, and some are the Rainbow Warriors. The women have been more consistent, all using Rainbow Wahine (wahine is Hawaiian for "women").

Stormy Petrels (Oglethorpe University, Georgia): The name refers to a plucky shore bird that dives straight into heavy surf to find its food.

Tarheels (University of North Carolina): There's a lot of history at UNC, the nation's first state university. A Tarheel is a North Carolinian, though some use it to refer to rural folk in general. The legend says that North Carolinian soldiers in Civil War Confederate service remained "stuck" to the ground as if they had tar on their heels. Inexplicably, the school uses a live ram as its mascot.

Warhawks (University of Louisiana–Monroe): One of college sports' newest mascots, the Warhawk represents the World War II fighter plane used by Louisianan Claire Chennault's American Volunteer Group in China, better known as the Flying Tigers. The logo, however, depicts a bird rather than a monoplane fighter.

 What are some of the greatest sports upsets?

A Athletes defying the odds and snatching victory from the jaws of defeat make for great stories (unless you're a fan of the competitor who was supposed to have the win safely sewed up). Here are some of the best.

1906 World Series: The Chicago White Sox defeat the crosstown Chicago Cubs. So what if the Cubbies won a record 116 regular season games that year?

1919: Man O' War: Whoa, big fella! The horseracing legend loses his only race to a 100–1 long shot. Almost too good to be true: That horse's name was Upset.

1951 New York Giants: One swing of the bat was all it took Bobby Thomson of the New York Giants to launch the "Shot Heard 'Round the World." The walk-off home run enabled the Giants to take the National League pennant from the Brooklyn Dodgers with a 5–4 win as announcer Russ Hodges screamed, "THE GIANTS WIN THE PENNANT!" (The Giants fell to the New York Yankees in the World Series, by the way.)

1959 Patterson–Johansson: Looking at the old photos, even Ingemar Johansson seemed shocked that he knocked down Floyd Patterson to claim boxing's heavyweight title in 1959. Patterson returned the favor the following year.

1969 Super Bowl III: Joe Namath and the New York Jets weren't supposed to get past the domineering Baltimore Colts. Everyone said so. Everyone was wrong as the Jets toppled the Colts 16–7.

1969 "Miracle Mets": The New York Mets had never finished better than ninth place prior to 1969—the year they won the National League division and championship playoffs, not to mention the World Series. Truly "Amazin' " stuff.

1974 Ali–Foreman fight: In 1974's "Rumble in the Jungle," George Foreman and Muhammad Ali squared off in Zaire for the World Heavyweight Championship. The bout was stopped in the eighth round, with Ali handing Foreman his first defeat.

1980 "Miracle on Ice: Who can forget the 1980 U.S. Olympic hockey team—a squad of collegiate athletes who defied the odds with a suspenseful 4–3 victory over their

Soviet Union opponents. Broadcaster Al Michaels' cry of "Do you believe in miracles?" still resonates. Oh, and for good measure, Team USA then captured a 4–2 victory over Finland in the gold-medal round.

1990 Douglas–Tyson: Mike Tyson was the undefeated heavyweight boxing champion in 1990. Then Buster Douglas delivered a punishing (and truly unexpected) defeat to the ill-prepared champ.

1990 World Series: The Oakland A's had won 103 games in the regular season, so it made sense that they would easily take the World Series crown. No one told the Cincinnati Reds that as they swept Oakland in four games.

1991 Final Four: Vegas odds-makers are still trying to explain Duke University's 79–77 win over top-ranked UNLV in the NCAA Final Four.

2000 Olympic Games: American wrestler Rulon Gardner defeated Russian Alexander Karelin, who had been undefeated for more than a decade.

2004 Boston Red Sox: The Red Sox win the World Series? Unlikely, since they were cursed by Babe Ruth. To make matters worse, they were down three games to none in the best-of-seven American League Championship Series (against the Yankees) and were trailing 4–3 in the bottom of the ninth. The rest is history as the BoSox later shocked the St. Louis Cardinals with a four-game sweep in the Fall Classic.

2005 Chicago White Sox: Perhaps inspired by the Red Sox, the White Sox took baseball's crown in 2005, snapping their 88-year drought.

2008 Super Bowl XLII: Poor Tom Brady. All he had left were good looks, a hot girlfriend, and lots of money after his New England Patriots fell to Eli Manning and the New York Giants. So much for the Pats' perfect season.

Q Who are the most underpaid athletes?

A With a question this wide open, it's easier to find an answer if you define the terms. Let's say, for the sake of argument, that the most underpaid athlete is the one whose earnings are the smallest relative to the revenue that his or her efforts generate. Let's consider the element of physical risk and wear-and-tear, too: The greater the demands of the sport, the more an athlete should be compensated. Let's also be open-minded about the nature of compensation: Some athletes don't care much about money; some, like horses, don't even know what money is. You get the idea.

It's popular to say that professional football players are underpaid. They make less on average than professional baseball, basketball, and even hockey players, yet the NFL is probably the most revenue-intensive athletic organization in the world. Only the opening ceremonies of the Olympic Games and the final soccer match of the World Cup tournament consistently outdraw the television viewership of the NFL's championship game, the Super Bowl. And because the game is so violent, NFL players tend to have short life spans—more than ten years shorter than that of the average American man, according to some studies. These guys are giving up a lot for their money.

Some folks like to say that major-college athletes are exploited. In 1999, the NCAA signed a six billion-dollar, eleven-year deal with CBS that allowed the network to broadcast the organization's basketball championships, yet no college athlete gets paid a dime. (Officially, that is.) But the exploitation argument is weak on several points. Many NCAA Division I football and basketball players get their college educations essentially for free. They also receive superior medical care, food, and housing, along with student-athlete-only tutoring and academic advisement, although universities don't tout this. Perhaps most importantly, these athletes make valuable connections for post-college careers, and the best of the bunch are trained to become millionaire pros in their chosen sport.

The bottom line is, you don't hear a lot of NCAA athletes complaining of the horrors of exploitation. They're too busy having the times of their lives, and they know that they'll graduate (if they bother to graduate) with a lot of advantages that their classmates never enjoy. Exploitation is in the eye of the beholder, you might say.

What about racehorses? Their industry is worth billions worldwide. Trainers, jockeys, racetracks, casinos, and gambling Web sites get rich off of their efforts while they risk death every time they gallop from the starting gate. Would you enter your neighborhood 5K if you knew that you might break an ankle and be euthanized within a few minutes of the starting gun?

No—but horses don't know about this. In fact, they don't know anything. They're horses. They like to eat and run, and stand around and eat some more when they're not running. That's their lives, apart from being put out to stud, which isn't a bad gig, either. Horses don't make any money, but they're rich in "life experience," as Oprah might say. If we judge them by human standards, they're exploited. But they're not humans.

Let's finish by returning to the human realm. Consider the late Colombian soccer player Andres Escobar, who was murdered by a fan in 1994 after he scored an own-goal that led to a 2–1 loss to the United States in the World Cup tournament. Think about the Iraqi athletes who were brutally tortured or killed by Saddam Hussein's son Uday after losing in the Olympics. The word "underpaid" doesn't begin to describe of these unfortunate athletes.

Q What's the difference between billiards and pool?

A It's a trick question: There is no difference. Billiards is a catchall term that includes a number of games that are played on a rectangular, felt-topped table and involve hitting balls with a long stick (the cue). Some of the more popular games include French (or carom) billiards, English billiards, snooker, and pocket billiards (which is the game you know as pool).

If you're a pool player accustomed to the satisfying clunk of a ball dropping into one of the pockets, French billiards will probably make you feel like you're in that weird, abstract foreign film that you were forced to watch on a bad date. There are no pockets, and there are only three balls: one white; one red; and one either yellow or white, with a little red dot on it. Either of the white balls (or the yellow ball) can serve as the cue ball. The point of the game is for the cue ball to hit the other two balls in succession. This is a carom. Each time a carom is accomplished, a point is awarded. The player who manages to keep from dying of boredom the longest is the winner.

English billiards incorporates the same three balls as French billiards, but the table has the six pockets familiar to pool players—one in each corner, and one on each of the long sides of the rectangle. There are four ways to score: You can hit the two balls in succession, à la French billiards; you can hit the red ball into a pocket; you can hit the other cue ball into a pocket; or you can hit the cue ball against another ball before the cue ball goes into a pocket. The winner is the player who can tally the score without using a slide rule.

The game of snooker also is played on a table with six pockets, but there are twenty-two balls: fifteen red balls, six balls of various colors that are assigned numbers, and a cue ball. After you knock a red ball into a pocket, you're allowed to pocket one of the numbered balls. The ball's number is added to your score, and then the ball is returned to the table. Then you have to pocket another red ball before going after a numbered ball, and so on. The winner is the player who can go the longest without giggling at any mention of the word "snooker."

Pocket billiards, or pool, involves fifteen numbered balls and a cue ball. Pool is played in bars, bowling alleys, and basement rec rooms across North America by people in various states of inebriation. Popular variations of pool include the games rotation, straight pool, and eight ball. Scoring systems differ, but the point of each game ultimately is to avoid finger injuries between games, when angry, drunken losing players engage in the time-honored tradition of venting their frustrations by hitting the remaining balls way harder than anyone would ever need to hit them.

Q How are tennis and handball related?

 Ever watch people playing handball and wonder, "Ow! Isn't that hell on their hands?" Well, it can be. That's why some players decided to take a different approach to handball, and used a racket instead. When you look back at the origins of tennis, you find handball at its root.

Interestingly, no one is quite sure exactly when tennis was invented. Some folks believe it's an ancient sport, but there's no credible evidence that tennis existed before A.D. 1000. Whenever the time period, most people can agree that tennis descends from handball.

The first reliable accounts of tennis come from tales of 11th-century French monks who needed to add a little entertainment to their days spent praying, repenting, and working. They played a game called *jeu de paume* ("palm game," that is, handball) off the walls or over a stretched rope.

The main item separating tennis from handball—a racket—evolved within these French monasteries. (The first rackets were actually used in ancient Greece, in a game called *sphairistike* and then in Persia, in a game called *tchigan*.) The monks had the time and means to develop these early forms of the tennis racquet: Initially, webbed gloves were used for hand protection, then paddles, and finally a paddle with webbing. The first balls were made from leather or cloth stuffed with hair, wool, or cork.

Once outside the cloister, the game's popularity spread across the country with the speed of an Amélie Mauresmo backhand. According to some sources, by the 13th century, France had more than 1,800 tennis courts. Most of the enthusiasts were from the upper classes. In fact, the sport became such a craze that some leaders, including kings and the pope, tried to discourage or ban the game as too distracting. Not to be torn from their beloved game, the people played on.

It didn't take long for tennis to reach merry olde England. There the game developed a similar following, counting kings Henry VII and Henry VIII among its fans. Even The Bard, William Shakespeare, refers to the game in his play *Henry V*, when Henry V is given a gift of tennis balls by the French Dauphin. At England's Hampton Court Palace, research suggests that the first tennis court was built there between 1526 and 1529. Later, another court was built, The Royal Tennis Court, which was last refurbished in 1628 and is still in use.

What's the difference between karate, kung fu, and tae kwon do?

Oh, this one is easy. Karate is the one that had its own movie, in which Arnold from *Happy Days* teaches Ralph Macchio how to wash a car while standing on one foot. Kung fu is the one that had its own TV show, in which a somewhat-Asian-looking hippie named Grasshopper roams the Old West, goading ornery, gun-slinging hombres into antagonizing him so that he can humbly murmur, "I do not wish to harm you," just before he unloads a saddlebag of hurt on them using only his hands and feet. And tae kwon do is the one that had its own radio show.

You don't remember *Tae Kwon Duo?* Every week, Dorothy Lamour and her faithful companion, Spud, patrolled the backstreets of a fictional Ohio metropolis called "Cleveland," selling War Bonds and vanquishing suspected Nazis with precisely delivered throat punches. They didn't make many episodes; the show was sponsored by the ill-fated Lucky Strikes Breakfast Cereal ("With extra nicotine for more pep!").

Okay, obviously some of that is made up. But to the casual observer, karate, kung fu, and tae kwon do can be difficult to tell apart. It's all just a bunch of barefoot dudes kicking each other, right?

The three disciplines do share similarities and have surely influenced each other over the centuries; each evolved in East Asia, after all. For clarity and a bit of simplicity, we can associate each discipline with a country: karate with Japan, kung fu with China, and tae kwon do with Korea. All are mainly unarmed forms of combat (although some styles of kung fu involve weapons) that are also practiced as sport or exercise and emphasize self-defense and spiritual development.

Karate stresses timing and coordination to focus as much power as possible at the point of impact. Blows are delivered with the hands, forearms, feet, knees, and elbows. At the height of his or her powers, a karate practitioner can split boards easily with a swift kick or punch.

Kung fu teaches self-discipline, with all of its moves beginning from one of five basic foot positions, most of which pay tribute to animals. Traditionally, kung fu places less emphasis on levels or rankings than the other two do (indicated, for example, by the different belt colors awarded in karate).

Tae kwon do is partially based on karate and features distinctive standing and jump kicks, but punching and blocking are also integral to it, just as they are to the other two disciplines. As in karate, students of tae kwon do often spar with each other; they try to avoid injury by learning to land their kicks and punches within inches of an opponent's body.

Each discipline requires years of study to master—but, despite what you may have learned from Hollywood, none involves much use of Turtle Wax.

Why do most sports go counterclockwise?

For most nonathletes living their quiet day-to-day lives, doing things clockwise seems pretty intuitive. Doorknobs turn clockwise, screws are tightened clockwise, and yes, clocks run clockwise. Board games usually move clockwise, blackjack dealers hand out cards clockwise, and people in restaurants usually take turns ordering in a clockwise direction. Yet in many of our sports, such as baseball and all types of racing, play moves in a counterclockwise direction. This can cause some serious confusion for clockwise-oriented individuals—just ask any T-ball coach trying to shepherd a young hitter down the first-base line.

How did this counterintuitive situation come to be? Part of the answer is rooted in history. In ancient times, when the Roman Empire ruled virtually the entire known Western world, a popular form of entertainment was chariot racing. As Charlton Heston fans know, chariot racing moved in a counterclockwise direction. Roman horses were invaluable in war and were trained to turn to the left to give right-handed spear-wielding riders an advantage in battle; in the Circus Maximus, it was natural to build the track to suit this. Considering the power of habit in human social development, it seems reasonable to assume that future forms of racing simply adopted the same direction of travel as the mighty Romans.

Some science-minded individuals postulate that foot racing goes counterclockwise due to physical forces. Because most people are right-handed (and right-footed), a counterclockwise motion tends to help those with a dominant right leg speed around turns. This is because of centrifugal force, which we're sure everybody remembers from high school physics. For those who have forgotten, centrifugal force is that sense of momentum—called inertia—that tries to keep you going in a straight line when you're trying to turn. A right-legged individual moving counterclockwise, this theory argues, will have a better chance of counteracting this force.

Some sports move the other way. In England, for example, horse races travel in a clockwise direction. This seems particularly baffling, considering that American horse racing—which was brought over by the British during colonial times—moves counterclockwise. It turns out, though, that counterclockwise horse racing actually developed in the United States in response to the British tradition. One of the first American horse tracks built after the Revolutionary War was established in 1780 by Kentuckian William Whitley. Flushed with pride at the newly won independence of the colonies, Whitley declared that horse racing in the new country should go in the opposite direction of those stodgy, tyrannical Brits.

Baseball, in which runners move counterclockwise around the bases, also may have descended from a British ancestor. Some baseball historians have postulated that the modern national pastime may be based on an older British bat-and-ball game called rounders. Interestingly, rounders players moved in a clockwise direction around the bases; why this was reversed in the rules of baseball is not known.

Possibly, the counterclockwise movement has to do with the orientation of the diamond. It's far easier for righthanders to throw across the diamond to first base if the runner is moving in a counterclockwise direction (which is also why you almost never see lefthanders playing any infield positions except for first base).

Of course, from one perspective, clockwise and counterclockwise are meaningless terms. Some physicists enjoy pointing out (somewhat smugly, we might add) that direction is entirely relative. Which means that those seemingly confused T-ball toddlers might be a lot smarter than we think.

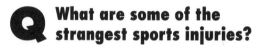

What are some of the strangest sports injuries?

 All athletes run the risk of injuries. Some of those injuries are just a little more unexpected than others...

Ryan Klesko: Unfortunately, sometimes it doesn't pay to be too patriotic. In 2004, this San Diego Padre was in the middle of pre-game stretches when he jumped up for the singing of the national anthem and pulled an oblique/rib-cage muscle, which sidelined him for more than a week.

Freddie Fitzsimmons: In 1927, New York Giants pitcher "Fat Freddie" Fitzsimmons was napping in a rocking chair when his pitching hand got caught under the chair and was crushed by his substantial girth. Surprisingly, he only missed three weeks of the season.

Clarence "Climax" Blethen: Blethen wore false teeth, but he believed he looked more intimidating without them. During a 1923 game, the Red Sox pitcher had the teeth in his back pocket when he slid into second base. The chompers bit his backside and he had to be taken out of the game.

Chris Hanson: During a publicity stunt for the Jacksonville Jaguars in 2003, a tree stump and ax were placed in the locker room to remind players to "keep chopping wood," or give it their all. Punter Chris Hanson took a swing and missed the stump, sinking the ax into his non-kicking foot. He missed the remainder of the season.

Lionel Simmons: As a rookie for the Sacramento Kings, Simmons devoted hours to playing his Nintendo Game Boy. In fact, he spent so much time playing the video game system that he missed a series of games during the 1991 season due to tendonitis in his right wrist.

Jaromir Jagr: During a 2006 playoff game, New York Ranger Jagr threw a punch at an opposing player. Jagr missed, his fist slicing through the air so hard that he dislocated his shoulder. After the Rangers were eliminated from the playoffs, Jagr underwent surgery and continued his therapy during the next season.

Paulo Diogo: After assisting on a goal in a 2004 match, newly-wed soccer player Diogo celebrated by jumping up on a perimeter fence, accidentally catching his wedding ring on the wire. When he jumped down he tore off his finger. To make matters worse, the referee issued him a violation for excessive celebration.

Clint Barmes: Rookie shortstop Barmes was sidelined from the Colorado Rockies lineup for nearly three months in 2005 after he broke his collarbone when he fell carrying a slab of deer meat.

Darren Barnard: In the late 1990s, professional British soccer player Barnard was sidelined for five months with knee ligament damage after he slipped in a puddle of his puppy's pee on the kitchen floor. The incident earned him the unfortunate nickname "Whiz Kid."

Marty Cordova: A fan of the bronzed look, Cordova was a frequent user of tanning beds. However, he once fell asleep while catching some rays, resulting in major burns to his face and body that forced him to miss several games with the Baltimore Orioles.

Sammy Sosa: In May 2004, Sosa sneezed so hard that he injured his back, sidelining the Chicago Cubs all-star outfielder and precipitating one of the worst hitting slumps of his career.

Jamie Ainscough: A rough and ready rugby player from Australia, Ainscough's arm became infected in 2002, and doctors feared they might need to amputate. But after closer inspection, physicians found the source of the infection—the tooth of a rugby opponent had become lodged under his skin, unbeknownst to Ainscough, who had continued to play for weeks after the injury.

Q What are some of the best nicknames in sports?

A The banter-filled atmosphere of the locker room, the media's fertile imagination, and fans' wisecracks give professional sports an inexhaustible source of interesting nicknames for teams, coaches, and players. Here are some of the most apt, colorful, and amusing.

Hockey

Stu "The Grim Reaper" Grimson (1988–2002; eight different NHL teams): One of hockey's tougher pugilists, six-foot-five Grimson earned more than 2,100 penalty minutes during his 729-game NHL career—with only 17 career goals. When asked how he reconciled his frequent fighting with his born-again-Christian faith, Grimson replied: "I don't think that Christ would be shy to shake off his gloves and protect his teammates."

André "Red Light" Racicot (1989–1994; Montreal Canadiens): For you non–hockey fans, the red light behind the net signals a goal—usually accompanied by a blaring siren or horn. For a goalie, being referred to as "Red Light" is like being called "Swiss Cheese" or "Sieve." But Racicot was nowhere near as lousy as his unfortunate nickname suggests. He won 26 games, lost 23, and tied 8 for the Canadiens, averaging 3.50 goals against per game—not All-Star stuff, but no reason for Racicot to hang his head.

Dave "Cementhead" Semenko (1977–1988; WHA and NHL Edmonton Oilers, NHL Hartford Whalers and Toronto Maple Leafs): During Wayne Gretzky's heyday with the great Edmonton teams, Dave had one job: Keep Wayne safe. Most players didn't rough up Gretzky, preferring to avoid being punched out by someone who once acquitted himself respectably in an exhibition bout with Muhammad Ali, as Semenko had.

Football

Dick "Night Train" Lane (1952–1965; Los Angeles Rams, Chicago Cardinals, Detroit Lions): Though this defensive wizard's tackles indeed felt like locomotive hits arriving out of the night, Night Train got the odd nickname from associating with fellow Hall of Famer Tom Fears, who constantly played the record Night Train on his phonograph. The name became so associated with Lane that today hardly anyone remembers his first name.

William "The Refrigerator" Perry (1985–1994; Chicago Bears, Philadelphia Eagles): The 326-pound "Fridge" took up a lot of space on the defensive line. But what brought him the most attention was Chicago coach Mike Ditka's willingness to use him at fullback on goal-line plays. Although he was considered quite formidable, this reputation was mostly media hype—Perry had only eight regular-season NFL carries for five yards and two touchdowns. Still, it was great fun for fans while it lasted.

Basketball

Darrell "Dr. Dunkenstein" Griffith (1980–1991; Utah Jazz): This doctor was only six-foot-four but could jump as though grafted to a pogo stick. Griffith grew up in the era of George Clinton's Parliament and Funkadelic bands, and his brother and friends gave him a nickname that rhymed with Clinton's Dr. Funkenstein character—hardly knowing it would become a household name when Griffith became a pro.

Vinnie "The Microwave" Johnson (1979–1992; Seattle Supersonics, Detroit Pistons, San Antonio Spurs): Basketball fans know how important the "sixth man" can be, and Vinnie was one of the best at coming off the bench. Boston Celtic Danny Ainge hung the tag on him in 1985 after Johnson's brilliant 34-point outing off the bench: "If that guy in Chicago is 'The Refrigerator,' then Vinnie Johnson is 'The Microwave.' He sure heats up in a hurry."

"Pistol Pete" Maravich (1970–1980; Atlanta Hawks, New Orleans Jazz, Utah Jazz, Boston Celtics): Had Maravich played his full career in the era of the three-pointer, there's no telling how many this deadly long-range gunner might have racked up. Pistol Pete's nickname evoked the quick-draw shooting threat he always was, but he was also a lot of fun to watch. He used his eerie peripheral vision to pull off hotdog passes and circus shots like one of the Harlem Globetrotters. The former gym rat died playing the sport he loved, suffering a heart attack when he was just 40 years old during a pickup game of three-on-three.

Baseball

Burleigh "Ol' Stubblebeard" Grimes (1916–1934; seven NL/AL teams): The last pitcher legally allowed to throw the spitball under the grandfather clause when baseball outlawed ball-doctoring, Burleigh always showed up with a faceful of scruffy whiskers. On the hill, he was meaner than a bag of bobcats, and he handily admitted this while wondering about all the "nice" guys in baseball.

Mike "The Human Rain Delay" Hargrove (1974–1985; Texas Rangers, San Diego Padres, Cleveland Indians): A lifetime .290 hitter, Hargrove got his nickname by fooling around in the batter's box: He would adjust his helmet, adjust his batting glove, pull on his sleeves, wipe his hands on his pants—and he'd do this before every pitch. If the pitcher threw instead to a base, Hargrove started screwing around all over again. Most pitchers like to get on with an at-bat, and it's probably no coincidence that Hargrove drew so many walks, intentional walks, and hits-by-pitch.

Pepper "The Wild Horse of the Osage" Martin (1928–1944; St. Louis Cardinals): Technically, "Pepper" was a nickname too. The Wild Horse of the Osage was born Johnny Leonard Roosevelt Martin. According to teammate Leo Durocher, Oklahoman Martin played commando-style ball on more than one level: He wore no underwear, much less a protective cup. His rather wild, free-spirited way of base-running got him the nickname, though it also probably referred to his love of practical jokes. Baseball historian Lee Allen summed up Pepper: "A chunky, unshaven hobo who ran the bases like a berserk locomotive, slept in the raw, and swore at pitchers in his sleep."

Chapter 2
EVENTS TO REMEMBER

Q **What scandal brought down the Louisville Grays?**

A The integrity of the game is of utmost importance in baseball. Unfortunately, that honor has not always been upheld. Perhaps the most famous scandal is that of the 1919 White Sox, in which eight players were banned from baseball for life after being accused of losing games for money. But while the Black Sox scandal has come to define the crime of game-fixing, that team wasn't the first to fix games. The first game-fixing scandal actually took place when the National League was barely a year old.

In 1877, the Louisville Grays were in first place when they headed on an Eastern road trip. On the trip, they made a number of suspicious errors that caused them to lose seven games and tie one. This prompted speculation that players dumped games, and cheated themselves out of the pennant that ended up going to Boston, quite intentionally.

It turned out they did. Western Union telegrams linked players with a known gambler, and four men—shortstop Bill Craver, pitcher Jim Devlin, utility player Al Nichols, and left fielder George Hall—were banned from baseball for life. Three of the men were banned based on the telegrams; Bill Craver was banned because he refused to co-operate with the investigation, which was taken as evidence of guilt. He also had past associations with gambling.

The Louisville Grays, who had only been founded in 1876, folded in 1877, and the men involved went on to a baseball-free future. (Ironi-cally, both Jim Devlin and Bill Craver would later find work in the law enforcement field, as police officers.)

Despite the publicity and punishments from the scandal, the years between 1877 and 1919 were hardly free of baseball corruption. First baseman Hal Chase served as its poster boy, having been linked to several "thrown" games before earning a ban for his role in the Black Sox scandal. There were attempts to bribe umpires (Bill Klem in 1908) and even official scorers (a 1910 attempt to get Cleveland's Nap Lajoie a batting title over the unpopular Ty Cobb). Suspicions that the 1914, 1917, and 1918 World Series were fixed were never proven, or perhaps the drama of 1919 would have been avoided. As it was, the eight White Sox players banned for life served notice that baseball was serious about keeping its games on the up-and-up.

Q How did Jeff Tarango make Wimbledon history?

A Despite its genteel history and emphasis on decorum, a good game of tennis can provoke on-court behaviors that are tyrannical or simply tiresome.

One such instance came in a match between Jeff Tarango and Al-exander Mronz at Wimbledon in 1995. Talk about mixed doubles!

During his third-round match against Alexander Mronz, the tennis menace Jeff Tarango put on a legendary display of spoiled sportsmanship, insolence, and all-round bad judgment. After chair umpire Bruno Rebeuh ruled against him on several close line calls, the feisty Tarango refused to continue the match, demanded that the accumulated throng watching the debacle "shut up," and accused the umpire of being "one of the most corrupt officials in the game."

At least one denizen in the crowd supported Tarango's view of the proceedings. His wife, Benedictine, strolled up to the on-court official and delivered an overhand smash of her own. She slapped the official twice across the face before storming out of the arena with her husband. Thus Tarango became the first player in Wimbledon history to default a match because of a disagreement over an official's judgment—not the kind of historical precedent most players want to set! Tarango was fined a record $15,500 for his tempestuous tirade.

Tarango was neither the first tennis player nor the last to lose his cool on the court at Wimbledon. In 1995, British player Tim Henman was disqualified from a match when, after missing a shot, he sent a ball careening away in anger. Unfortunately a ball girl in its path was struck in the head.

And then there's John McEnroe, who was famous for his tantrums; The New York Times once dubbed McEnroe "the worst advertisement for our system of values since Al Capone." In a 1981 Wimbledon match against Tom Gullikson, in addition to his usual repertoire of ranting, raving, and racquet launching, McEnroe immortalized his rebellious reputation by continuously shouting, "You cannot be serious!" at umpires and line judges. This behavior continued throughout the duration of the tournament, and despite winning the prestigious prize for the first time, McEnroe was not offered a membership to the All-England club, an honor usually afforded to every first-time victor. But at least McEnroe got a title for his later autobiography out of the incident—he titled it *You Cannot Be Serious*.

Q Which teams were involved in the football play known as "The Immaculate Reception"?

A The outcome looked blacker than bleak for the Pittsburgh Steelers as the clock wound down on their 1972 AFC divisional playoff clash with the Oakland Raiders. Sequestered on their own 40-yard line, down by a single point, bereft of time-outs, and facing a seemingly insurmountable fourth and ten, the Steelers certainly looked like they needed supernatural intervention to win. And then a miracle was delivered.

With 22 seconds left, Steelers pivot Terry Bradshaw evaded an onslaught of Oakland pass rushers, twisted, turned, and tossed a pass toward receiver Frenchy Fuqua, who was just about to haul in the ball when he was blindsided from behind by Raiders safety Jack Tatum. The ball sailed over the flattened Fuqua, plunked Tatum on the top of his shoulder pads, and caromed wildly into the air, actually moving backward as it plunged toward the pitch. Incredibly, it was caught by Pittsburgh running back Franco Harris, who scooped up the cascading ball just before it hit the ground and trotted untouched the length of the field for the touchdown that gave the Steelers a 12–7 lead.

After considerable debate, including a call from the field to the press box for a rule clarification, the play was allowed to stand, sealing a Steelers win. Since Bradshaw's pass was thrown on a wing and a prayer, Franco's catch was enshrined in the lexicon of legends under the heading, "The Immaculate Reception."

Q What teams played in the first college football game broadcast on the Big Ten Network?

A The teams were the Appalachian State Mountaineers and the University of Michigan Wolverines, and the people who tuned in got a rather large surprise.

The Wolverines, members of the top-tier Football Bowl Subdivision (FBS), were expected to win easily against the Mountaineers, members of the Football Championship Subdivision (FCS). Generally, when teams from the FCS played teams from the FBS, they were expected to lose, playing the game in order to gain exposure and revenue for their school's athletic departments. But the Mountaineers motored onto Michigan's home turf and pulled off what many pundits hail as one of the biggest upsets in the history of American sports, much less college football. After a late field goal propelled the Mountaineers into a 34–32 lead, Michigan marched down the field, eventually setting up a seemingly simple 27-yard three-pointer for the win. However, Appalachian defender Corey Lynch blocked the kick to secure the Mountaineers' victory.

It was the first time that an FCS team defeated a ranked FBS team.

Q Which team used a "College of Coaches"?

A For Chicago Cubs fans in the early 1960s, the question wasn't "Who's on First?," but rather, "Who's in the dugout?"

If ever there was an idea that deserved a failing grade, it would be Philip K. Wrigley's College of Coaches.

The Chicago Cubs were once one of baseball's elite teams. But that was many years in the past; by 1961, the team hadn't had a winning record for over a decade. This was despite the presence of some good ballplayers on the roster, most notably Hall of Famers Ernie Banks and Billy Williams.

Cubs fans had put up with a lot as the team struggled for years under owner Philip K. Wrigley, the gum magnate who had inherited the team in 1932. Once, for example, Wrigley traded his team manager for another team's broadcaster.

But that was nothing compared to what Wrigley concocted in 1961. Scrambling for a new strategy, he unveiled not one new manager that season, but eight. Wrigley had devised a bizarre new system that he called "The College of Coaches."

Here's how it worked: From a pool of coaches, Wrigley would select one to be the head coach, or manager, for an unspecified period of time. Then, whenever he felt like it, Wrigley would pick a new head coach from the pool.

The concept behind the College of Coaches was that instead of firing the manager if the team played poorly, Wrigley could merely demote him and immediately choose a replacement from seven others rather than spend long hours searching for a new manager. He also intended for the coaches, during the times they were not the head coach, to work with the players to instill a cohesive system and style. Therefore, whenever a new head coach was appointed, the players would already know the system.

The idea received a storm of ridicule. "The Cubs have been playing without players for years," said one critic. "Now, they're going to try it without a manager."

Undeterred, Wrigley and the Cubs sailed into the 1961 season on the good ship College of Coaches—and promptly began listing to one side. The experiment violated a cardinal rule of successful sports teams: Consistency is vital. Under the College of Coaches, the players never knew who was going to be in charge, or for how long. The comfort and security a player felt under one manager might be yanked away the next day when a new man took over.

In addition, the other coaches weren't always inclined to help the existing head coach if things went bad, preferring to wait until they got their own shot at the top job. With each head coach set in his own way of doing things, chaos reigned in the Cubs dugout.

In 1961, the first year of the College of Coaches, the team finished four games better than they had the previous year. But in 1962, the Cubs' ship really sank as the team went 59–103, finishing the season ahead of only the hapless New York Mets, who lost a record 120 games that year.

In 1963 and 1964, Wrigley kept up the pretense of rotating coaches, although he kept one man in charge all year. In November 1965, the system mercifully came to an end. Although Wrigley Field was famous for its ivy-covered outfield walls, Wrigley's experimental "college" was anything but Ivy League.

The College of Coaches had flunked out.

Q What children's movie interrupted coverage of a 1968 Jets-Raiders game?

A Most football fans know of the 1968 "Heidi Bowl," when NBC shifted coverage in the Eastern time zone from a great Jets-Raiders contest (that still had more than a minute to play!) to a made-for-TV movie of the children's classic *Heidi* at 7:00 P.M.

The network had scheduled three hours for the game in the Eastern markets, which seemed sufficient—at that time, NBC hadn't shown any professional football games that ran longer. As 7 P.M. approached, however, it became clear that the game would run long. Some people began to call their stations to urge the network to complete the game, while others enquired as to whether *Heidi* would start on time. In fact, irate New York callers actually blew fuses on the switchboard at the local NBC station. When they couldn't get through to the network anymore, they called the police.

To make things worse, the Jets, who had the lead when the broadcast was terminated (32–29), managed to lose when the Raiders scored two touchdowns in that final minute! The final score was 43–32 in favor of the Raiders.

After the incident, it became standard practice for networks to let games finish before moving to scheduled programming.

Q What year did an earthquake interrupt the World Series?

A The real drama at the 1989 World Series had nothing to do with baseball. It came instead from Mother Nature, which produced an earthquake that measured 6.9 on the Richter

Scale (7.1 surface-wave magnitude), claimed more than sixty lives, and injured thousands. Technically, the earthquake that rocked San Francisco at 5:04 P.M. on October 17, 1989, was the Loma Prieta Earthquake. But it's known as the World Series Earthquake.

The Oakland A's and San Francisco Giants, Bay Area neighbors, were squaring off for the ultimate prize. While people in the region were affected by the quake no matter what they were doing, the nation experienced the tragedy through the eyes of World Series television cameras. ABC Sports play-by-play man Al Michaels was reading taped highlights during the Game 3 pre-game show when millions across the country heard him utter the words, "I'll tell you what—we're having an earth—..."

Screens went black. When backup power was restored, the images were powerful. Among them: chunks of concrete falling from an upper deck section of Candlestick Park; Commissioner Fay Vincent looking dazed after nearly being knocked out of his seat near the Giants' dugout; players from both teams leading their wives and children onto the field, away from the stadium's walls.

Though the old stadium shook, the walls held, and no one inside was seriously hurt. Some players clung to their families on the field, thankful for their safety. Others remained lighthearted, not knowing the severity of the damage outside the stadium. It was only on their way home that many people learned they had just survived the area's strongest quake since the 8.3 monster of 1906.

The Series resumed ten days later with a tribute to those who had lost their lives. A moment of silence was observed at 5:04 P.M., followed by the singing of "San Francisco," an unoffical city anthem. The ceremonial first pitch was thrown by representatives of public safety and volunteer organizations who responded to the disaster. Oakland then completed a bittersweet sweep on a stage that wound up being far more about life than baseball.

 What time did the 1985 Mets-Braves game on Independence Day finish?

 The 1985 Mets–Braves game lasted nearly seven hours and featured 29 runs and 46 hits over 19 innings.

It was getting late on July 4, 1985, at Atlanta's Fulton County Stadium. Rick Aguilera was scheduled to start for the New York Mets the following night against the Braves, so the pitcher returned to his hotel room for some rest. When he woke up at 3:00 A.M. and saw the Braves–Mets baseball on his TV, Aguilera assumed it was highlights from the game and went back to sleep. Never in his wildest dreams would he have imagined his teammates were still playing. But they were.

It was the game that wouldn't end, which was a shame for those among the 44,947 in attendance who were there mainly for the Independence Day fireworks after the game. First, there were two rain delays. Then when the Mets took a 10–8 lead in the 13th and it appeared the end was at hand, the Braves scored twice in the bottom of the inning. New York took another lead in the 18th, but a home run by Braves reliever Rick Camp extended what had already become the longest game in major-league history.

Camp, however, gave up five runs in the top of the 19th. Atlanta scored twice in the bottom of the frame, but the time had come to surrender. The Mets won 16–13, recording the final out at 3:53 A.M. after six hours and ten minutes of play.

New York's Keith Hernandez hit for the cycle. The Mets pounded out a club-record 28 hits. Only one position player, third-string Mets catcher Ronn Reynolds, did not get in the game. New York's Darryl Strawberry and manager Davey Johnson were ejected in the 17th inning for arguing balls and strikes. They were outlasted by about 8,000 fans.

As a reward to those who stuck it out, the Braves decided to go ahead with the fireworks—to the dismay of those who lived near the ballpark. Several Atlanta residents awoke to what they thought were gunshots at just past 4:00 A.M.

"It probably wasn't the best game I ever played in," said Braves third baseman Ken Oberkfell, "but it certainly was the oddest."

 What caused Babe Ruth's "Bellyache heard 'round the world"?

A Let's face it, it wasn't exactly the "Shot heard 'round the world." But because it was Babe Ruth, the "Bellyache heard around the world" carried some importance. But what happened?

Babe Ruth was, and remains, one of the most famous baseball players in history. It was Ruth's prodigious slugging in the early 1920s that saved baseball from the Black Sox Scandal. It was also his presence on the New York Yankees—a formerly mediocre team—that turned them into a collection of world-beaters.

In his first few seasons with the Yankees, Ruth set home run records and drove the team into the World Series three years in a row (1921-1923). The Yankees won the series in 1923, and even though they missed out in 1924, there was every expectation that they'd be back in 1925—after all, they had Babe Ruth. But no one counted on the Bellyache Heard Around the World.

Although he was reportedly fighting the good exercise fight on his farm in Sudbury, Massachusetts, Ruth, who never met a meal he didn't eat, had ballooned to 245 pounds over the winter. Prior to spring training in early February 1925, Ruth went to Hot Springs, Arkansas, to get in shape for the coming season. Besides its therapeutic mineral baths, Hot Springs was also known as a pre-Vegas Vegas. Before long, Ruth was fully caught up in two of his favorite pastimes: sex and food. To combat his stomach's protests over the large amount of chow he was shoveling in, Ruth gulped bicarbonate soda to settle his belly. However, there was no such remedy for whatever sexual diseases were floating around. As contemporary sportswriter Fred Lieb noted: "One woman couldn't satisfy him. Frequently it took half a dozen."

Needless to say, Ruth was badly out of shape when spring training started in St. Petersburg, Florida. By late March he was struggling with "lame legs." But that hardly stopped the Ruthian caravan of food and sex. As teammate Joe Dugan later commented, "He was going day and night, broads and booze."

As the Yankees made their way north from spring training to start the season, Ruth got progressively worse. Finally, on April 7, Ruth collapsed at the train station in Asheville, North Carolina. Rumors spread like wildfire that the Sultan of Swat was dead; a London newspaper vividly reported the death scene. Ruth revived, only to collapse again in the train bathroom, smashing his head against the sink. When the train reached New York, the unconscious Ruth (estimated at 250-270 pounds) was hoisted out through the train window. At the hospital, Ruth was delirious and convulsing. On April 17, he had a very hush-hush operation.

For decades, the story given to explain Ruth's illness was one invented by sportswriter W. O. McGeehan, which combined rambunctiousness with aw-shucks innocence: Ruth had simply eaten too many hot dogs, peanuts, and soda. That's just so All-American it has to be true, right?

There are other stories. Long after Ruth's death, his wife Claire wrote that he had suffered a groin injury. Perhaps, but groin injuries normally don't cause their subjects to become delirious. Another possibility is gonorrhea—a rumor believed by several teammates and even Yankee General Manager Ed Barrow. Yet while Ruth's liaisons with anything wearing a skirt could certainly have given him a STD, surgery would have been an unusual treatment.

This leaves the possibility that Ruth had what one of his physicians called an "intestinal abscess." Ruth biographer Marshall Smelser speculated that Ruth likely had an obstruction of the intestine, requiring a temporary colostomy. In those days, such a personal and private procedure would not have received mention in the press.

Most likely, we'll never know the full truth. That year was Ruth's worst season in baseball, but soon he was back to boozing and whoring. As his roommate "Ping" Bodie allegedly said when asked what it was like to room with Ruth, "I ain't rooming with Ruth. I room with his suitcase."

Q What are the greatest team turnarounds in baseball?

 When all is said and done, baseball is a game of streaks. Even the worst hitter gets hot for a game or two; even the best puts together a 2-for-30 at some point. What separates the champion from the others is that the champion has more "up" streaks than "down" and keeps them going longer.

Every so often, a team manages to turn their fortunes around, digging themselves out from a huge deficit. Here are the tales of four teams that traveled a long way during the course of one season to finish first, including some that fought back from the verge of elimination to become world champs.

The Team: 1914 Boston Braves
The Deficit: 15 games behind first-place Giants on July 4
The Comeback: 68–19 after July 4

The Braves had lost one hundred games or more four years in a row when George Stallings was hired as manager for the 1913 season. Their fifth-place finish that year was a welcome delight, but the team started 1914 back in the cellar and was languishing there as late as the Fourth of July.

Traveling home after a road trip, the Braves stopped for an exhibition game against the minor-league Buffalo team. They got trounced 10–2, which was a serious wake-up call for Stallings's crew. They made their move, thanks in part to near-perfect pitching by 27-year-old Dick Rudolph (who went 18–1 the second half of the season) and 22-year-old Bill James (17–1) and great infield defense from new kid Rabbit Maranville at short and old hand Johnny Evers at second. Manager Stallings relied on platooning to maximize his offensive strength, and his team roared from last place to first in just thirty-seven days.

In early September, Stallings conjured up another marvel by starting an inexperienced hurler (who had made only 21 big-league appearances through 1914) named George Davis against the Phils. The spitballer twirled a no-hitter. And once the Braves moved past the Giants, there was no stopping them. They finished the season 10½ games ahead of John McGraw's men. Then they jumped into the World Series and swept Connie Mack's Philadelphia A's in four games. No wonder they became known as "The Miracle Braves."

The Team: 1951 New York Giants
The Deficit: 13½ games back on August 11
The Comeback: 37–7 in the final 44 regular-season games

By 1951, the Giants and the Dodgers had been adversaries for decades. So when the Dodgers swept a three-game series at Ebbets Field from their rivals to take a huge 12½-game lead on August 9, they were in a celebratory mood. Knowing they could be heard in the visiting clubhouse, they began to sing, "Roll out the barrel! We've got the Giants on the run!" Jackie Robinson used a bat to bang out the beat on the door between the clubhouses.

Then Leo Durocher's Giants kicked it up a notch. The Dodgers didn't play badly, but the Giants played amazingly well. At one point, they won 16 games in a row. The Dodgers still had a seven-game lead on September 1, but the relentless Giants squeezed into first place on the next-to-last day of the season, and the Dodgers had to win a 14-inning nail-biter against the Phillies to set up the three-game playoff.

In the first game, Giants third baseman Bobby Thomson hit a home run off Dodger pitcher Ralph Branca to give his team a 2–1 lead and eventual 3–1 win. Game 2 was a 10–0 Dodger cakewalk. In Game 3, Branca returned to the mound to face Thomson again, trying to hold a 4–2 Dodger lead with two men on—but Thomson attacked a Branca fastball and lined it into the lower deck of the Polo Grounds' left-field seats. The sensational Giants' two-month upswing was capped by this incredible comeback. Thomson and Branca are forever linked in myth and memory, and Thomson's homer became known as "The Shot Heard 'Round the World."

The Team: 1978 New York Yankees
The Deficit: 14 games back on July 18
The Comeback: The Yanks beat the Boston Red Sox in a one-game playoff to advance to the postseason

The 1978 Red Sox were a force to be reckoned with. Led by slugger Jim Rice, who would finish the season leading the league in hits, triples, homers, total bases, and RBI, they pounded the ball. By mid-July they were more than 30 games over .500, leading Milwaukee by 9 games and the Yankees by 14.

Yankee owner George Steinbrenner couldn't abide scurrilous comments by Yank manager Billy Martin, who resigned midseason and was replaced by the mellow Bob Lemon. The effect on the team was immediate. By mid-August the Yanks had taken 10 out of 12. Then they won 12 out of 14. As the Sox fell prey to an assortment of injuries, the Yankees kept up the pressure, capped off by a four-game September sweep in Fenway Park in which the Yanks outscored the Sox 42–9. The Boston press dubbed it "The Boston Massacre."

In only about seven weeks, the Yankees had chewed up the 14-game difference and moved into a 3½-game lead. But the Red Sox fought back, winning their final eight regular-season games to force a one-game playoff at Fenway. Yankees shortstop Bucky Dent, who had belted a total of five home runs all year, stepped up to the plate in the seventh and slugged a three-run shot over the Green Monster in Fenway's left field. The Yankees' huge comeback was complete. To this day Boston fans consider "Bucky Dent" a vile epithet.

The Team: 2004 Boston Red Sox
The Deficit: Down three games to none in the American League Championship Series
The Comeback: Four straight wins, including two in extra innings

The Red Sox seemed to be a team trapped by history. Many a rabid Bostonian believed in "The Curse of the Bambino," which claimed that the Sox were doomed never to win the World Series because they had the gall to sell the greatest player of all time, Babe Ruth. So when the team began the 2004 American League Championship Series by dropping three in a row to their archrivals, the New York Yankees, few expected them to overturn history's applecart.

To get an idea of the scale of the mountain the Sox had to climb, consider that in 36 League Championship Series and 95 World Series, no team had ever come back from a 3–0 deficit to win a best-of-seven series. In fact, in the twenty times a team had taken a 3–0 lead, only three times did their opponents even win Game 4.

But these Red Sox called themselves "the idiots," because their all-out style of play didn't leave time for fretting over historical matters. The Sox were competitive in Games 1 and 2, although they wound up with losses in both, but they got absolutely clobbered in Game 3 (19–8).

Game 4 should have been the clincher for the Yanks. In fact, they were three outs away from sweeping the Series when suddenly the Sox roared back. Boston rallied against their longtime nemesis, Yank reliever Mariano Rivera, in the ninth inning and won on a

David Ortiz homer in the 12th. The next night it took 14 innings for the Bostonians to eke out another win, this time also on an Ortiz RBI. He fouled off six pitches in a ten-pitch at-bat before he got the one he could knock out of the park. In Game 6, Curt Schilling rose to the occasion on a surgically patchworked right ankle (his tendon was temporarily sewn into place) and delivered seven heroic innings as the Sox tied the Series at three in what is now known as the "Blood on the Sock" game. Then Boston blew out the Yanks and rewrote history with a 10–3 victory in Game 7. They kept it rolling, sweeping the World Series in four games over the St. Louis Cardinals.

Chapter 3
GETTING INTO GEAR

Q **What is the uniform for underwater hockey?**

A Invented in 1954 by Alan Blake of England, underwater hockey evolved over the years into an international sport. The first world championship was held in 1980, with only a handful of teams competing; in 2013, teams from nineteen countries competed in a variety of events at the World Championships in Hungary.

Rules are similar to traditional hockey, but the equipment varies greatly between the two sports, with the most obvious changes being to the sticks and pucks. Since underwater hockey requires that its participants push the puck along the bottom of a pool, the disc is suitably hefty, weighing about three pounds. (In fact, they're sometimes made of lead.) On the other hand, the stick is a wimpy device, approximately one foot long.

Aside from the obvious differences in playing surfaces, another major distinction between ice hockey and underwater hockey is the uniforms. Ice hockey players layer up with heavy padding and clothing, but underwater hockey players must don a different set of equipment before they submerge themselves in water. Gear is designed both for protection and for aerodynamic movement through the water. Players need an aerodynamic, non-baggy swimsuit, fins, a snorkel, a cap, a glove for their playing hand, and a diving mask. The cap is the same kind as is worn in water polo, and it protects the player's eardrums. Referees generally wear red caps and orange gloves to identify themselves.

Incidentally, if you prefer creative names, you might want to spend time in Great Britain, where the sport still sometimes goes by its original name: Octopush. The name comes from the fact that in the early days, there were eight players on a team, pushing the puck around. (Nowadays, only six players from a team can be in the water at once.) To match the underwater theme, the puck was called a "squid."

Q Who makes the metal whistles used by referees?

 What do a police officer directing traffic, a football referee calling a foul, and a schoolteacher trying to keep students under control have in common? If they're using a whistle, it was probably manufactured by the American Whistle Corporation.

Based in Columbus, the American Whistle Corporation is the only metal whistle manufacturer in the United States. And it takes its product seriously—in certain circumstances, a loud whistle can save lives. The company was founded in 1956 as Colsoff Manufacturing and was purchased by its current owner, Ray Giesse, in 1987. It currently manufactures more than a million chrome-plated brass whistles a year for clients that range from municipal police departments to the referees who officiate at the Super Bowl.

Whistles from AWC have been found in some truly unique places, including the wedding of Giesse's daughter. To commemorate the event, Giesse produced 230 custom whistles, each stamped with a heart and the names of the bride and groom. Guests received their whistles at the reception, resulting in an almost deafening din.

A lot goes into the production of an AWC whistle. According to the company's Web site, the process begins with coiled brass, 30-ton presses, and state-of-the-art soldering tables; and continues with polishing and specialized plating. Lastly, a tiny ball made of synthetic cork is stuffed inside each whistle.

AWC whistles are the loudest commercial whistles available—at least four decibels higher than those of their competitors, according to company PR. Whistle lovers can join the thousands who have toured the company's manufacturing plant by calling AWC and reserving a spot.

Q How do corked bats help cheating baseball players hit the ball farther?

A In this age of performance-enhancing drugs, it's almost refreshing when a hitter gets caught cheating the old-fashioned way. Corked bats somehow recall a more innocent time.

There are different ways to cork a wooden baseball bat, but the basic procedure goes like this: Drill a hole into the top of the bat, about an inch in diameter and twelve inches deep; fill the hole with cork—in rolled sheets or ground up—and close the top with a wooden plug that matches the bat; finally, stain and finish the top of the bat so that the plug blends in.

The supposed benefits of a corked bat involve weight and bat speed. Cork is lighter than wood, which enables a player to generate more speed when swinging the bat. The quicker the swing, the greater the force upon contact with the ball—and the farther that ball flies. The lighter weight allows a batter more time to evaluate a pitch, since he can make up the difference with his quicker swing; this extra time amounts to only a fraction of a second, but it can be the difference between a hit and an out at the major league level.

Following the logic we've set forth, replacing the wood in the bat with nothing at all would make for an even lighter bat and, thus, provide more of an advantage. The problem here is that an empty core would increase the likelihood that the bat would break; at the very least, it would cause a suspicious, hollow sound upon contact with the ball. The cork fills in the hollow area, and does so in a light-weight way.

Not everyone believes that a corked bat provides an advantage; some tests have indicated that the decreased bat density actually diminishes the force applied to the ball. But Dr. Robert Watts, a mechanical engineer at Tulane University who studies sports science, sees things differently. He concluded that corking a bat increases the speed of the swing by about 2.5 percent; consequently, the ball might travel an extra fifteen to twenty feet, a distance that would add numerous home runs to a player's total over the course of his career.

In any case, we haven't heard much lately about corked bats. That's because the headlines have been dominated by players who have used steroids to cork themselves.

Q Why are there stripes on bowling pins?

A As any modern-day hipster can tell you, bowling is more about fashion than rolling a ball into a rack of pins. So perhaps it's not surprising that even bowling pins pay homage to the style gods. With a pair of sweet stripes like an ascot around its neck, a bowling pin resembles a 1950s Frenchman on a yacht trip off the Riviera.

Okay, so maybe bowling pins aren't inspired by haute couture. (But don't try to tell us those shoes aren't!) Actually, bowling pins are a classic case of form following function. It's been a long evolution: Archaeologists have found evidence of bowling pins dating back almost two thousand years. Those first bowling pins were made of stone, but by the late nineteenth century, bowling-pin manufacturers had turned to maple as their material of choice. These early pins were made from a solid block of wood, but problems with splintering and uneven weights led to inconsistent pin behavior and lower scores than bowling's governing body at the time, the American Bowling Congress (ABC), liked to see.

Pin manufacturers eventually discovered that gluing pieces of maple wood together and coating them with a synthetic lacquer not only made it easier to produce pins with more consistent weights, but also resulted in a sturdier pin. Pins are still generally made from maple, despite experiments with steel, plastic, and even magnesium.

Nowadays, all bowling pins are standard-ized according to specifications set by the United States Bowling Congress (or USBC, as the former ABC is now known). These specifications include height and weight measurements, as well as the circumference of different parts of the pin. Nowhere in the specs, however, is there a mention of stripes, though the USBC does allow for pins to have "neck markings."

So why stripes? According to representatives of both the USBC and Brunswick Bowling, there is no particular reason. The convention of striping first appeared early in the twentieth century, as bowling's popularity grew and companies began mass-producing bowling equipment. These stripes were nothing more than a form of decoration—a stylistic flourish.

Stripes aren't the only bits of flair to appear on pin necks. For example, Brunswick manufacturers some pins with crowns around the necks. We, however, are partial to the image of ten Frenchmen in ascots. It's way more fashionable.

Q Why is a football shaped that way?

 Would you rather call it a bladder? Because that's what footballs were made of before mass-produced rubber or leather balls became the norm.

The origins of the ball and the game can be traced to the ancient Greeks, who played something called *harpaston*. As in football, players scored by kicking, passing, or running over the opposition's goal line. The ball in *harpaston* was often made of a pig's bladder. This is because pigs' bladders were easy to find, roundish in shape, relatively simple to inflate and seal, and fairly durable. (If you think playing ball with an internal organ is gross, consider what the pig's bladder replaced: a human head.)

Harpaston evolved into European rugby, which evolved into American football. By the time the first "official" football game was played at Rutgers University in New Jersey in the fall of 1869, the ball had evolved, too. To make the ball more durable and consistently shaped, it was covered with a protective layer that was usually made of leather. Still, the extra protection didn't help the pig's bladder stay permanently inflated, and there was a continuous need to reinflate the ball. Whenever play was stopped, the referee unlocked the ball—yes, there was a little lock on it to help keep it inflated—and a player would pump it up.

Footballs back then were meant to be round, but the sphere was imperfect for a couple reasons. First, the bladder lent itself more to an oval shape; even the most perfectly stitched leather covering couldn't force the bladder to remain circular. Second, as a game wore on, players got tired and were less enthused about reinflating the ball. As a result, the ball would flatten out and take on more of an oblong shape. The ball was easier to grip in that shape, and the form slowly gained popularity, particularly after the forward pass was introduced in 1906.

Through a series of rule changes relating to its shape, the football became slimmer and ultimately developed its current look. And though it's been many decades since pigs' bladders were relieved of their duties, the football's nickname—a "pigskin"—lives on.

Why do golfers wear such silly clothes?

A In most of the major sports, athletes don't have much choice when it comes to what they wear. Basketball, football, baseball, and hockey teams all have uniforms. But other athletes aren't so lucky (and neither are their fans). Golfers, for example, are allowed to choose their own garb, leading to a parade of "uniforms" that look as if they were stitched together by a band of deranged clowns.

Why big-time golfers wear such hideous clothes is a source of bewilderment. Some apologists blame it on the Scots. Golf, after all, was supposedly invented by shepherds in Scotland back in the twelfth century, and it almost goes without saying that a sport born in a country where man-skirts are considered fashionable is doomed from the start. We'd like to point out that we are no longer in twelfth-century Scotland—let's move on, people.

But history may indeed play a role in golf's repeated fashion disasters. Kings and queens were reputed to have hit the links in the sixteenth and seventeenth centuries, and by the late nineteenth century, golf was a popular pastime amongst the nobility of England and Scotland. The nobility, however, wasn't exactly known for its athletic prowess. The other "sports" many of these noblemen participated in were activities like steeplechase (which has its own awful fashion), and so most early golfers had no idea what types of clothes would be appropriate for an athletic endeavor. Early golfers simply took to the links wearing the fashionable attire of the day—attire that, unfortunately, included breeches and ruffled cravats (these were like neckties).

The tradition of wearing stuffy, silly attire continued into the twentieth century (as did the tradition of wealthy, paunchy white guys playing the sport), with awful sweaters and polyester pants replacing the ruffled cravats and knee-length knickers. Yet, remarkably, modern golfers take umbrage at the stereotype that duffers have no sense of fashion. According to one golf wag, the knock on

golfers for being the world's worst-dressed athletes is unfair because nowadays almost everybody wears Dockers and polo shirts.
(We'll pause while that gem sinks in.)

To be fair, the dreadful golf fashions of the 1970s and 1980s have
given way to a more benign blandness that is at least less offensive, if not remotely what anybody would call "stylish." Of course,
all fashion is less offensive than it was in the 1970s and 1980s, so
perhaps golf fashion is proportionally no better.

"Golf," Mark Twain once complained, "is a good walk spoiled."
We love Mark Twain, but we have to say that spoiling a good
walk is the least of golf's transgressions.

Q What's inside a baseball?

 Though nearly every red-blooded American child has
thrown one, hit one, or broken a neighbor's window with
one, there are few who know what a baseball has beneath its
white outer skin and trademark red laces. As it turns out, there is
little inside the orb aside from string and a bit of rubberized cork.

Official Major League baseballs are assembled in Costa Rica, but
their materials come from the United States. A baseball begins
as a 2.06-centimeter sphere that is made of a cork-and-rubber
composite and is subsequently surrounded by two rubber layers,
the first black and the next red. By the time both inner and outer
covers are molded on, the circumference of the ball has grown to
10.47 centimeters. The core, or "pill," of the baseball is manufactured in Alabama. The next layers to be applied are the windings,
which are made of wool from Vermont and poly/cotton. The wind-

ings are applied in four layers and bring the ball's circumference to 22.52 centimeters.

The white outer shell that we all know and love is made of cowhide from Tennessee. More precisely, it is Number One Grade, alum-tanned, full-grained cowhide that, for the most part, comes from Midwest Holstein cattle. Preference is given to this type of hide because of its smooth, clean surface area and uniform grain. (Only the best when it comes to America's pastime.) After the cover is added, the completed official baseball measures between 22.86 and 23.49 centimeters in circumference.

The final ingredient is 223.52 centimeters of waxed red thread, which is used to create 108 stitches. Each completed baseball must weigh between 141.75 and 148.83 grams. That's about an ounce heavier than a quarter-pounder with cheese, as weighed prior to cooking—the burger, not the ball.

Q Why would you want to put "English" on the cue ball?

A Pool is a game with a long history. Also known as pocket billiards (which distinguishes it from carom billiards, snooker, and other billiard games that are played on pocketless tables), pool was once seen in a negative light because it was associated with seediness, drinking, and gambling. (In short, trouble—right here in River City.) Although it's still popular to play pool in bars—and to bet on the outcome—pool tables have migrated toward respectability, becoming staples of rec centers and family basements.

Pool seems fairly simple at first glance, whether you're playing eight-ball, nine-ball, or any of the game's countless other variations. Of course, you need some basic skills—for a beginner, for example, it might be difficult to even hit the cue ball without ripping up the felt. But once you've got the basics down, you'll notice that the simple rules of geometry govern the motion of the pool balls when they bounce off of each other or the side rail. Knowledge of these rules allows a competent player to predict the exact route that the ball will take on the table.

And this is where "English" comes in. Putting English on the ball is a way to momentarily suspend the laws of geometry and to change the predicted outcome when the cue ball hits the rail or another ball. It's done by striking the cue stick slightly off-center—the ball still travels in a straight line, but it has spin on it, which changes the effect of its impact.

If you put left or right English on the ball, it changes the angle that it takes when it bounces off the rail—and it changes the angle that the other balls take when they get hit. You can also give a ball "follow" or "draw." If you put follow on the cue ball, the topspin will cause it to follow after the ball that it hits; if you use draw on the cue ball, the spin will bring it back toward you after it hits its target. There's also "stop," which makes the cue ball freeze after it bangs into another ball.

Why is it called English? It's only called that in the United States; cue-ball spin is known as "side" in England, where the technique was invented. English manufacturers started adding tips to cues in the early eighteen hundreds. Not only did the tip enable the player to make better contact with the cue ball, but it also allowed for deflection. English pool players who visited the United States demonstrated their mastery by making seemingly impossible shots—and inspiring their slack-jawed American opponents to call the technique "English."

If you want to improve your pool game, learning how to put English on the cue ball is one way to do it. But the cat's out of the bag—unlike when those British pool sharks visited America, everyone now knows about English, so don't expect to impress anyone with your sneaky technique.

Q Why do baseball players wear knickers?

 Some call them knickers. Others call them short pants. Either way, there's nothing short about the answer, which stretches about one hundred and fifty years into the past. Back then, baseball was evolving into a professional sport, and there was a lot of innovation going on regarding the game's equipment. This even included the players' pants.

The long, baggy—almost dressy—pants that players wore in the mid-eighteen hundreds proved suboptimal where a player's speed and agility were concerned. They simply got in the way. Some players innovated by having buttons sewn at the hem so the pant legs could be cinched tight. Other teams had straps on their pants. The Cincinnati Redlegs cut to the chase in 1868 by showing up one April day in honest-to-god knickers—the better to show off their red stockings, too.

Incidentally, this wasn't the only innovation the Redlegs brought to baseball. One year later, the Redlegs became the first openly all-professional baseball team. A year after that, their catcher invented the baseball glove—or at least became the first prominent ballplayer to use one.

The concept of a professional ballplayer has evolved since those days, and so have gloves—enormously. But interestingly, knickers stayed the norm for almost a century, until near the mid-twentieth century, when Carl Hubbell, Ted Williams, and others started to wear their pants in the "low-roll" style—that is, rolled into their uniform stockings around midcalf. It's entertaining to imagine the stir that caused, especially when we think of the disapproval that current-day heel-length trousers elicit from baseball purists. Ballplayers have always been vain about their pants, apparently.

Today, pant legs are all over the board. Some players wear them Redlegs style, right under the knee. Others wear them like the ballplayers of one hundred and fifty years ago, down to the ankle (but these are a good deal more form fitting on the way down the leg). Major League Baseball's 2002 collective bargaining agreement stipulates no pants past the tip of the shoe heel, for some measure of neatness in appearance. But the fact is, pant length is one of the areas of true sartorial creativity in baseball today, whether a player chooses to wear knickers or not.

Q Who was the first hockey goalie to wear a mask?

A Gruesome facial injuries to two legendary hockey goalies spurred the invention and acceptance of the goalie mask. Yet despite the hazards posed by playing without a mask, the face-saving innovation took a long time to catch on.

Today, it's hard to fathom a hockey goalie playing without a mask. Indeed, all pro and amateur hockey leagues now require the mask to be part of a goalie's equipment. But for the first nine decades of hockey's existence, the goalie mask was an object as odd and rare as the U.S. two-dollar bill.

As crazy as it sounds, goalies actually chose not to wear masks despite obvious occupational hazards. Not surprisingly, then, the introduction and popularization of the goalie mask only came about after a near-tragedy involving two of the game's greatest netminders.

Clint Benedict played 18 pro seasons with the Ottawa Senators and Montreal Maroons, backstopping the Senators to Stanley Cup titles in 1920, 1921, and 1923, as well as helping lead the Maroons to their first Cup win in 1926. Arguably the best goalie of his era, Benedict revolutionized how the position was played. He earned the nickname "Praying Benny" due to his habit of falling to his knees in the era of the stand-up goaltender. As a result, the NHL eventually abandoned its rule prohibiting goalies to leave their feet.

In 1930, Benedict inadvertently led to yet another innovation to the goal-tending profession. That year, in a game between the Maroons and the Montreal Canadiens, the Canadiens' Howie Morenz nailed Benedict in the face with a shot that knocked him unconscious, shattered his cheekbone and nose, and hospitalized him for a month. When Benedict returned to the ice to face the New York Americans, he surprised the crowd by sporting a leather mask, making history as the first goalie to wear face protection in an NHL game.

After five games, Benedict fatefully discarded the mask, saying its oversize nosepiece hindered his vision. Shortly after, another Morenz shot struck Benedict in the throat and ended his NHL career. Amazingly, for the next 29 years, the first man to wear a mask in a game would also be the last.

The mask finally reappeared in 1959—albeit unexpectedly—in a game between the Montreal Canadiens and the New York Rangers. Three minutes into the game, Rangers star Andy Bathgate drilled the Canadiens' all-star goalie Jacques Plante in the nose and cheek with a hard shot, sending a badly bleeding Plante to the dressing room. Plante had been wearing a fiberglass mask in practices since the mid-1950s, but Montreal coach Toe Blake forbade him to don it in a game. Now, as Plante was being stitched up, he told the coach he wouldn't go back on the ice without his mask. An irate Blake, faced with no suitable backup goalie, was forced to relent.

Plante returned to the game wearing his mask and led the Canadiens to a 3–1 victory. Montreal subsequently reeled off an 18-game unbeaten streak, with a masked Plante in net for every game. The goalie mask was here to stay. Within a decade, it became commonplace throughout hockey.

On April 7, 1974, the Pittsburgh Penguins faced off against the Atlanta Flames as the 1973–74 National Hockey League regular season drew to a close. Playing in goal for the Penguins was a 30-year-old journeyman named Andy Brown.

Brown turned in a sievelike performance, and the sad-sack Penguins were thrashed 6–3. Worse yet, the loss turned out to be the last game of Brown's NHL career. But as he braved pucks whizzing past his head, Brown staked his place in hockey history: He would be the last goalie to play in an NHL game without a goalie mask.

Q **What's the job of a golf ball diver like?**

A Remember the time you duck-hooked three consecutive tee shots into the lake before finally hitting a lousy eighty yards into deep rough? What happens to that layer of golf balls at the bottom of the lake? They're fished out by a golf ball diver—check out the following interview with a golf ball diver for answers to questions you didn't even think to ask.

Q: How many balls does a golf ball diver fish out of a water hazard in a day?

A: At a large course, probably 2,000 or more. That's assuming I don't die in the process. In many parts of the United States, golf ball diving is an extreme sport.

Q: Because you get hit with golf balls?

A: No, though it does happen. Because I can drown, or have an encounter with an alligator, or get bit by a water moccasin—I have lots of hazards of my own. Leeches attach to me. Turtles have tried to take off my fingers. Even some fish think I'm food.

Q: Come on. Most of these lakes are less than ten feet deep, and you're fully qualified in scuba and wearing scuba gear. How could you drown?

A: You'd be sad to see how easily a diver, especially one carrying a big netlike bag full of golf balls in a dark environment, can get hung up in weeds along the bottom of a lake. I could be down there struggling to get free, running out of oxygen, while ten yards away

Joe Duffer is celebrating because he just hit the green in regulation for the first time in a week. If I panic, I'm dead. The only way I live through that is if I can remain calm and methodically get myself loose.

Q: Okay, but alligators and snakes? Don't most golf courses remove dangerous reptiles?

A: In Southern states, these critters are everywhere. I don't know of any gator that can read "no trespassing" signs. Usually, where there's water, there are alligators and snakes.

Q: Threatening animals aside, how do you manage to find balls in the dark water?

A: By feel. I can't wear gloves, which is dangerous. I curse the people who have thrown beer bottles into a water hazard to a life of four-putts, because I've been cut quite a bit. I also find a lot of other junk, and stuff that's not junk. I've recovered quite a few golf clubs, often really expensive ones.

Q: Do you make good money?

A: I can. You have to love to dive, and you have to be able to work alone, because unlike the usual dives, you aren't with a buddy. I get a few cents a ball, but that adds up. Sometimes I find specialty balls that sell for a lot more—souvenir balls, really expensive premium balls. One time I pulled out a ball with the presidential logo. If I can get paid to go diving, I don't mind the occasional leech bite.

Q What gear do people need in the sport of zorbing?

A Straight from New Zealand comes zorbing, an offbeat ball sport invented in the 1990s. To zorb, you need a giant plastic ball, a friend or assistant that you trust quite a bit, and enough space to roll. Here's the drill: The zorbian (zorbing enthusiast) straps himself inside a fully inflated plastic ball. Some of the balls have harnesses inside, while others do not. Generally the ball is made of two layers: the person is inside the inner layer, while a cushion of air fills the outer layer.

Once a person is secure, common sense is jettisoned in favor of high adventure, and the assistant sets the ball rolling, usually down some kind of hill. Happy shrieks can be heard as the zorbian attains speeds up to 25 miles per hour.

If the ball veers off course or takes a bad bounce, shrieks of a far different sort can be heard.

Clearly on a roll, this sport has spread into Norway, Sweden, Switzerland, China, Japan, England, and the United States, among other countries.

Q Why do baseball managers and coaches wear uniforms instead of street clothes?

A Coaches in basketball, football, hockey, and soccer are content to wear street clothes, and some, such as Pat Riley in the NBA, have even garnered extra respect for their sartorial strategies. Yet managers and coaches in baseball dress just like the players. What gives?

More than any other sport, baseball clings to its traditions—not unlike the way a stretchy polyester uniform clings to the expanding midsection of an aging manager. Despite such modern phenomena as free agency, domed stadiums, and sausage races, today's baseball culture still has roots in the game's distant past. In the nineteenth century, ball clubs really were clubs—fraternities that played baseball by day and gathered at night for formal parties, where players ate, drank, socialized, and sang special club songs. The uniforms they wore were almost sacred articles that distinguished the players not only from those of rival ball clubs but also—and perhaps more importantly—from spectators and the rest of society at large.

In those early days, the captain of the team held the responsibilities of a modern-day manager: creating lineups, making key tactical decisions, and kicking dirt on the shoes of an unsympathetic umpire. As the game evolved and the century turned, the more successful captains found work as managers after their playing days were over. But since they were unwilling to surrender their membership in the fraternity of baseball, they continued to wear their uniforms.

There were exceptions—most famously, Connie Mack, who managed the Philadelphia Athletics for a preposterously long time, from 1901 to 1950. A former major-league player, Mack nevertheless wore a suit and tie when he managed the A's. Perhaps not coincidentally, Mack also owned the franchise, so his ties to the fraternity were likely not as strong as those of most managers.

There are some practical considerations. Many baseball coaches spend time on the field before the game instructing players, leading them in warm-ups, and hitting ground balls to infielders—all of which would be difficult to accomplish in a suit and tie. What's more, the official rules of Major League Baseball stipulate that first-

and third-base coaches should be in uniform. There's no mention of the manager, though; in fact, rule 3.15 states, in part, "No person shall be allowed on the playing field during a game except players and coaches in uniform, managers, [and] news photographers." The rule book seems to be saying, indirectly, that the manager doesn't need to be in uniform.

But an incident in 2007, during which a representative from the baseball commissioner's office harassed Boston Red Sox manager Terry Francona during a game for not complying with the league's dress code (Francona sometimes preferred to wear a Red Sox pullover instead of the regulation uniform top), suggests that today's baseball uniform remains every bit as sacred as the sausage race.

Q Who invented the jockstrap?

A On November 28, 2005, the Bike Athletic Company celebrated the production of its 350 millionth jockstrap, which was promptly framed and flown to the company's headquarters. Let's take a closer look at some landmarks in the long history of this piece of men's protective underwear.

The origin of the jockstrap begins in 1874, thanks to Charles Bennett, who worked for the Chicago-based sporting goods company Sharp & Smith. Originally, Bennett designed his garment to be used by bicyclists in Boston. In 1897, Bennett and his newly formed BIKE Web Company (as Bike Athletic was known then) officially patented his invention.

At the time, a bicycle craze was sweeping the nation. These bikes weren't like today's average cruisers; instead, the bicycles of yore were high-wheeled and quite precarious. Folks raced these bikes around steeply banked velodrome tracks as well as through Boston's bumpy cobblestone streets. The daredevils on the velodromes were known as "bike jockeys," which led to Bennett naming his invention the "BIKE Jockey Strap," later shortened to "jockstrap." Two decades later, the U.S. Army issued jockstraps to World War I soldiers in order to reduce "scrotal fatigue." When the troops came home, the bicycle craze had been replaced by the rough and tumble sport of football; the jockstrap found a new home on the gridiron.

To most men of a certain age, the jockstrap is a right of passage that signals the arrival of puberty and a need to protect the male reproductive organs during vigorous exercise. To the uninitiated (or women), the jockstrap might contain some mystery, but its construction is rather simple. A jockstrap (or athletic supporter) consists of an elastic waistband and leg straps connected to a pouch that holds the testicles and penis close to the body, sometimes with the added plastic cup (ostensibly to avoid injury). The original design, with the addition of the cup, hasn't changed much since the early 1900s. FYI, jockstrap size refers to waist size. In this case, bigger isn't necessarily better.

In 1974, the jockstrap turned 100 years old, but the anniversary was a quiet one—alas, no national magazine covers commemorating the garment, no ticker-tape parade. Perhaps it was due to a national feeling of modesty, yet 15 years later, as a journalist writing for the *Orlando Sentinel* remarked, a certain women's undergarment—the bra—received plenty of press for its centennial. In fact, when the bra turned 100, *LIFE* magazine issued six pages to celebrate, along with a pictorial, and a headline shouting "Hurrah for the bra." Ten years later, as the jockstrap turned 125, a *Houston Chronicle* writer wondered why we'd forgotten about the forsaken jockstrap.

Perhaps we'd been too distracted by Y2K in 1999, he wrote, or maybe "the jock just isn't in the same league [as the bra]....A bra suggests female mystery; a jock suggests male vulnerability."

In the past few decades, there has been some run on jockstrap territory by the likes of the more free-flowing boxer shorts, jockey shorts, and, for athletic types, "compression shorts." Slowing numbers can be pointed to increased competition, or perhaps men are acting out against years of ridicule by classmates and less-than-tactful gym teachers. Still, after more than 130 years on the market, the jockstrap probably isn't going anywhere just yet.

Chapter 4
GRAB BAG

Q What sport might lugers do in warm weather?

A Most Americans think about the sport of luge once every four years, when the Winter Olympics make an appearance on our television sets and people pause to try to remember what the difference is between luge and skeleton. (Both are sled-based events. In luge, the lugers compete while lying face up, and they hurtle down the track feet first, reaching speeds of up to 90 mph, or 140 km per hour. In skeleton, by contrast, competitors lie face down and plunge down the track headfirst.) Luge may not have the highest profile in America, but the sport has been around since the late 1800s, and it was first included in the Winter Olympics in 1964.

If you'd like to try luge but don't have a track nearby, or want to ease into things, you can look into street luge. Street luge (aka land luge, road luge, or butt-boarding) is where speed freaks go when the melt is on. As with winter luge, the first to reach the bottom wins. Unlike the snowy version, street luge uses steep paved roadways of varying lengths for propulsion.

Street lugers lay flat on their backs, but because there is no ice, they ride an elongated version of a skateboard. Steering is accomplished with leg pressure and by shifting body weight.

Born in Southern California in the 1970s by skateboarders searching for greater speed, a modern "boarder" can hit speeds in excess of 70 miles per hour, with handling that boggles the mind. Even so, accidents happen, and when they do, they're generally spectacular.

Q What stadium is referred to as "The House That Doak Built"?

A There was a time when athletic achievement was measured by integrity, intelligence, and on-field accomplishments rather than bank balances, contract clauses, and off-field romances. The undisputed star of this era was a humble, honest, and hard-hauling running back from Southern Methodist University named Doak Walker, a perpetual All-American who became so popular that the Cotton Bowl Stadium was resized to seat all the spectators who scrambled to see him soar and score.

It's been written that Doak Walker was so shifty that he could evade tacklers in a phone booth, so humble that he wrote thank-you notes to the scribes who regularly chose him as an All-American, and so popular that he appeared on the cover of 47 major magazines during his illustrious years playing for the SMU Mustangs and NFL's Detroit Lions. Not content to limit his athletic talents to the gridiron, Walker also lent his skills to the SMU basketball and baseball teams. However, it was on the football field that the Dallas native excelled and evolved.

Walker attended Highland Park High School in Dallas, where he shared the sporting spotlight with future NFL Hall of Fame quarterback Bobby Layne. After graduating in 1944, Walker stayed close to home and attended SMU, where he tore up the turf for the Mustangs in various roles: as a star halfback, defensive back, punter, and kick returner.

Walker's athletic prowess, combined with SMU's on-field success and a soaring spectator interest, forced the Mustangs to relocate their home games to accommodate the crowds they drew. The team moved from Ownby Stadium, located at the south end of the SMU campus in the University Park neighborhood in Dallas, to the larger Cotton Bowl Stadium at the Texas State Fair. The stadium, which sat more than 40,000 fans, was also the home of the annual Cotton Bowl Classic, a postseason match that pitted a Texas team against an independent school.

Founded in 1937, the Cotton Bowl game was a financial liability in its early years, rarely attracting sellout crowds despite the presence of a hometown host, and often losing money. In 1941, the powers that be decided that the champion of the Southwest Conference (SWC) would host the annual Cotton Bowl game, but the advent of World War II and a drop in the quality of competition continued to undercut the showcase.

However, once Doak Walker and the Mustangs became the park's regular tenants during the season, attendance soared and interest intensified. Walker, who solidified his standing among the all-time gridiron giants by winning the 1948 Heisman Trophy, led the SMU team to a pair of Cotton Bowl game appearances, including a title-winning victory over Oregon in 1949. He was named MVP in both his Cotton Bowl games.

Almost 30,000 seats were added to the stadium to meet the demand for tickets, raising its capacity from 46,200 to 75,504. This could only help to promote the prestige and popularity of the game, which became a nationally followed favorite. Walker's role in the ascension of the game and the stadium that hosts it up to full-fledged classic status was solidified when scribes began referring to the Cotton Bowl as "The House that Doak Built," placing Walker's name alongside Babe Ruth's as athletes whose acclaim transcended the playing field.

The SMU Mustangs continued to use the Cotton Bowl stadium as their home turf until 1979, when the school moved its home games to Texas Stadium, home of the NFL's Dallas Cowboys. The House that Doak Built saw its most enduring tenant, the Cotton Bowl Classic, host its final game in the stadium in 2009, as plans were made for the bowl game to relocate to the new Cowboys Stadium in Arlington beginning in 2010.

Q Can a woman take a man seriously who brings a cowbell to a football game?

A Men don't have a monopoly on spectator sports—plenty of women love to watch the games, too. A study that was published in the *Journal of Sport Behavior* revealed some findings that might be surprising: In a random sampling of men and women, the percentage of self-proclaimed sports fans within each gender was nearly equal, and men and women reported spending roughly the same amount of time attending live sporting events.

But be honest: If you take a moment to conjure a picture in your head of the stereotypical crazy sports fan-donning face paint, a wacky wig, and a full uniform, you don't imagine a woman. You see a man.

The common perception is that the most disturbingly devout sports fans are men, and the research supported it. When subjects of the study that was published in the *Journal of Sport Behavior* were asked about the amount of time they spend talking about sports or watching sports on TV, or about how strongly they identify themselves as sports fans, the guys kicked butt across the board. And they probably high-fived each other about it later.

"Females [attend sporting events] for social reasons. When the game's over, the game's over," says Miami University social psychologist Beth Dietz-Uhler, who helped conduct the study. "But men get so much of their identity from sports."

And that identity often manifests itself in behavior that most men would never display anywhere outside of a sports arena. A lot of male sports fans—even the ones without the cowbells—feel like they have a personal stake in the game, as if they can somehow affect the outcome by worrying about it or by making noise in the stands. This likely stems from a lifetime of active participation in sports.

So women don't need to worry. Deviant sports-fan behavior among men is not (necessarily) an indicator of deeper personality flaws. Many of the men in the stands simply feel compelled to do something, anything, in an attempt to feel like they're part of the action on the field.

"In reality, fans don't have any impact on the outcome of the game," says Christian End, a Xavier University social psychologist who also worked on the study. "Just because the team has lost doesn't mean you're a loser as well."

Try telling that to the poor schmuck who's moping through the parking lot with tear-streaked face paint dripping onto his cowbell.

Q What president tried to have a troublesome tree removed from a golf course?

A A number of our nation's presidents have been sportsmen: Gerald Ford played football in his youth; Theodore Roosevelt hunted, fenced, played polo, wrestled, and boxed; Barack Obama plays pick-up basketball. John Quincy Adams liked to swim—specifically, he swam naked in the Potomac River. (Apparently when you're age 60-something and the president, you can get away with such things. Just don't get caught. According to political legend, a reporter found Adams during a skinny-dipping jaunt and refused to let him out until the president granted him an interview.) Many presidents have hit the golf course, swinging a club with varying degrees of ability.

So it really isn't shocking that someone like Dwight D. Eisenhower—a former U.S. Army general and the 34th U.S. president—might want to unwind with a game of golf. It's a very presidential thing to do. And Ike probably thought that rank had its privilege when he requested (in 1956) that a tree at Augusta National be removed because it was interfering with a few of his drives.

Augusta National Golf Club, however, did not comply with the request. But due to the request, the tree, a pine on the 17th hole, took on the nickname of the "Eisenhower Tree." It challenged competitors at the Masters Tournament for many more years, until 2014, when an ice storm caused so much damage that the tree had to be removed.

Q What sports have been traditionally associated with Christmas in America?

A When many people gather together, games often abound. Whether it's a snowy round of capture the flag on the lawn, a board game marathon, or classic hide-and-seek with the kids, Christmas is a time for play. Here are some of history's traditional Christmas games you might consider adding to your family's holiday game repertoire.

Blindman's bluff: When the plain old game of tag got boring, someone came up with blindman's bluff, a fun variation. The game is simple: Whoever is "it" is blindfolded. That person then gropes around the room, trying to make contact with the other, nonblind-folded players—who try not to get caught. This game was popular during Henry VIII's reign and has been a holiday favorite for many years, especially for young people during the Victorian era.

Stoolball: In 1621, the governor of the British Colony of Mas-sachusetts ordered the citizens of Plymouth to stop playing games on Christmas Day, deeming it an unholy way to observe the Lord's birthday. One of the rowdy games he put an end to was stoolball. The game went like this: A milking stool was used as a target, and a hard leather ball stuffed with either hair or feathers was thrown at it. One player pitched the ball; another defended the stool with a bat made of wood. Sound familiar? This game evolved over the years to something we call "baseball."

Pitching the bar: This was another Christmastime game Puritan leaders put a stop to, at least for awhile. "Pitching the bar" was es-sentially a game of strength, where the typically male players would heave a log over their shoulder, similar to events in logger games today. The guy who pitched the log the farthest won. Since there was lots of wood chopped for the winter season, this game was particularly popular during the colder months, and that meant it was a Christmas favorite.

Football, rugby, and their relatives: Football has been around since at least the Middle Ages, but as tough as it is today, it was nothing compared to what it was like back then. There were few rules, the "field" was usually the whole town, and games often dissolved into bitter fistfights and brawls. Basically, it was loosely organized chaos, which may be why it remained a popular sport through the ages. Many football games were organized around the Christmas holidays, since peasants and serfs had the rare opportunity to put down their work and spend time in leisure.

Riding the stang: The first colleges in America were the birthplace of plenty of games and pranks, and the Christmas holiday brought out the rowdiest of diversions. In addition to ballgames and pranks played on teachers, students at schools such as Cambridge would make a tiresome classmate "ride the stang." That meant he would have to sit on a pole that was carried by the rest of his class as they traveled throughout campus, laughing and poking fun at him. Not the nicest game in the world, but fun if you weren't the one on the pole.

 **Is golf a sport?**

A Look it up in any dictionary: "Sport" is generally defined as recreation, a competition based on skill, and a pleasurable activity. No dictionary makes any exceptions regarding the participants' bloated midsections, their lack of perspiration, or their absurd pants. You can argue until you're blue in the face, but it comes down to semantics, and golf fits the bill.

Some might argue that the frustration that accompanies four hours on the links isn't the least bit pleasurable, but how many of us would find pleasure in getting crushed by a three-hundred-pound defensive tackle? Lack of pleasure doesn't prevent us from calling football a sport, so there's no point in trying to trip up golf on this technicality. Even if we sometimes wonder why a jittery, exhausted nineteen-year-old kid can sink a pair of game-winning free throws as fifty thousand people scream at him during the NCAA's Final Four, while a comfortable, filthy-rich, forty-something golfer demands perfect silence every time he tries to hit a ball that is sitting absolutely motionless on a tee.

Still, we can't argue with the dictionary. Golf is a sport.

Why not blame the inventors of this infuriating pastime instead? For years, the Scots have taken the credit. And who better to hold responsible for such a game than a bunch of miserable haggis eaters? But historical research shows that plenty of folks in many ancient cultures spent hours out in the fields pointlessly hitting balls with sticks. In the end, it looks as though the Dutch may have the closest claim. The stick in their stick-and-ball game was called a *kolf* or *kolve*.

 ## Was professional wrestling ever real?

 If it ever was, nobody's letting on now. In its current golden age, professional wrestling has learned to flaunt its spurious side, and fans just keep eating it up. World Wrestling Entertainment, Inc., the outfit that rules big-time pro wrestling, is a multimillion-dollar operation with shares traded on the New York Stock Exchange.

Pro wrestling was born in the humbler surroundings of the carnival circuit of the nineteenth-century, where strongmen would take on local challengers who paid for the chance to get into the ring and fight for prize money. The matches were fixed—sometimes with the help of the challengers and sometimes not. In any event, crowds loved the drama, and it wasn't long before the promoters realized that the challengers' entry fees were peanuts compared to the money that could be made by charging admission for folks to watch the matches.

During several peaks in wrestling's popularity—such as the 1930s, 1950s, and 1980s—everyone involved swore that the fighting was real. Wrestlers adhered to a code called "kayfabe," which is an old carnival term that means, essentially, "fake." If a wrestler stepped out of character, flouted the script, or otherwise undermined the illusion that the events were real, he was breaking kayfabe. And anybody who broke kayfabe in wrestling was not long for the sport.

This is not to suggest that wrestlers aren't athletes. A pro wrestling match is like a dangerous, brute-force ballet, and the performers have to be in excellent shape to pull off all of their moves. Pro wrestling has even gone through its own steroids scandal, just like any other sport.

As for the nagging "real" thing, that's not even a question anymore. In its high-finance, twenty-first-century incarnation, professional wrestling has openly embraced the notion that the matches are staged. Think of these matches as soap operas with knee drops.

How high can you legally dribble a basketball?

There are numerous rules on how to properly dribble a basketball, but bouncing the ball with such force that it bounds over the head of the ball handler is not illegal.

Although it might fun-up the standard NBA game to see players drumming dribbles with the exaggerated effort of the Harlem Globetrotters, it wouldn't do much to move the game along. And contrary to popular belief, there is no restriction on how high a player may bounce the ball, provided the ball does not come to rest in the player's hand.

Anyone who has dribbled a basketball can attest to the fact it takes a heave of some heft to give the globe enough momentum to lift itself even to eye-level height. Yet, the myth about dribbling does have some connection to reality. When Dr. James Naismith first drafted the rules for the game that eventually became known as basketball, the dribble wasn't an accepted method of moving the ball. In the game's infancy, the ball was advanced from teammate to teammate through passing. When a player was trapped by a defender, it was common practice for the ball carrier to slap the sphere over the head of his rival, cut around the befuddled opponent, reacquire possession of the ball, and then pass it up court. This innovation was known as the overhead dribble, and it was an accepted way to maneuver the ball until the early part of the 20th century. The art of "putting the ball on the floor" and bouncing it was used first as a defensive weapon to evade opposing players.

By the way, there is absolutely no credence to wry comments made by courtside pundits that the "above the head" rule was introduced because every dribble that former NBA point guard Muggsy Bogues took seemed to bounce beyond the upper reaches of his diminutive 5'3" frame.

Q Does a curveball really curve?

A The curveball has been baffling hitters for well more than a hundred years. Hall-of-Famer William "Candy" Cummings is credited with being the first pitcher to master the curve, which he began throwing with great success in 1867 as a member of the Brooklyn Excelsiors. Anyone who has stood in a batter's box and faced a pitcher with an effective curve will tell you that the ball is definitely doing something unusual.

Yet for almost as long as pitchers have been buckling batters' knees with the breaking ball, a small contingent of naysayers has maintained that the ball does not curve, and that the whole thing is an optical illusion. Before the availability of advanced photographic technology, various tests were performed by those curious enough to want to know the truth. Pitchers threw curveballs around boards, through hoops, and parallel to long rods. In 1941, *Life* magazine did a photographic analysis of a curveball and concluded that, no, the ball does not actually curve. The same year, however, *Look* magazine did its own tests and drew the opposite conclusion.

Today's super-slow-motion TV technology catch curveballs in the act all the time, and it sure looks like the ball is curving. And the truth is, a curveball does curve. Physicists have said so, decisively. They can even tell you the name of the principle that makes it curve: the Magnus effect.

A pitcher who throws a curveball snaps his wrist when he throws, creating a high rate of topspin on the ball. As the ball travels, the air passing on the side against the spin creates drag and higher pressure, while the air passing on the other side has no drag and the pressure is lower. The higher air pressure on one side effectively pushes the ball toward the low-pressure side, sometimes a foot or more. That's the Magnus effect.

The force of gravity also comes into play. Because a curveball is thrown at a slower rate of speed than a fastball, the curve will drop more noticeably than a fastball as it approaches the batter. The combination of the curve and the drop makes it difficult to predict where the ball will be once it reaches home plate and, thus, con-founding to hit.

There's even an equation to figure out how much a ball will curve. It looks like this: FMagnus Force = KwVCv. This may seem compli-cated, but we're willing to bet that for most people, it's still easier to solve the curveball equation than it is to hit the curveball.

Q Shouldn't the Los Angeles Lakers be called the Oceaners instead?

A They probably should be, given the team's proximity to the Pacific Ocean and the conspicuous lack of lakes in the Los Angeles area. But it's not that simple. For those of you who don't know anything about the history of the National Basketball Asso-ciation (NBA) before Michael Jordan, here's a lesson. The Lakers didn't originate in Los Angeles—they came from Minneapolis, where they were, in the 1950s, the NBA's first dynasty.

Actually, the team that became the Lakers started in Detroit, as the Gems of the National Basketball League (NBL), a predecessor of the NBA. Ben Berger and Morris Chalfen purchased the franchise in 1944 and moved it to Minneapolis three years later. They renamed the team "Lakers," an acknowledgement of Minnesota's status as the "Land of 10,000 Lakes."

Since the Gems were the worst team in the NBL in the 1946–47 season, the Lakers got the first pick in a dispersal draft of players from the defunct Professional Basketball League of America, which earned them the rights to George Mikan, the first "greatest" player in pro basketball history. With Mikan, the Lakers won the NBL title in 1948; jumped to the Basketball Association of America and won its title in 1949; then joined the newly formed NBA and won titles in 1950, 1952, 1953, and 1954. But the booming Los Angeles market was too tempting to resist, especially considering that attendance dropped significantly in Minneapolis after Mikan retired following the 1953–54 season, and so the Lakers became the NBA's first West Coast franchise in 1960.

As for the matter at hand: No, it doesn't make sense to call a Los Angeles team the Lakers. The only lake of significance around the city is north of the downtown area, at Echo Park. But we're not going to pick on L.A.'s basketball team for being associated with a lake instead of an ocean. At least not until the NBA's Utah Jazz return their incongruous and ludicrous nickname to the city where they originated, New Orleans, and adopt something more area-appropriate—like the Slalom, the Flats, or the Mormons.

Who's the guy on the NBA logo?

A No matter where you are in the world, there is a symbol that almost everyone recognizes. For many people, it represents not just the American sport of basketball, but also all of American sport—and in some ways, perhaps America itself.

No, we're not talking about the Air Jordan logo. We're referring to the NBA logo—you know, the white-silhouetted player who is driving to the hoop over a background of red and blue. But as recognizable as the logo is, you'd be hard-pressed to find many people who can name the guy after which it is modeled.

Well, that guy is Jerry West. Even though most younger fans of the game may think of West as a silver-haired director of basketball operations who represented the Memphis Grizzlies at various draft-lottery drawings, West is one of the greatest guards to ever play the game.

Known as "Mr. Clutch," West averaged twenty-seven points a game during his fourteen-year career with the Los Angeles Lakers. West was an all-star fourteen times, earned several nods to the NBA all-defensive team, and was an All-Star Game and a Finals most valuable player. But more than his statistics or awards, his silky-smooth movements were what prompted NBA logo designer Alan Siegel to model his 1969 design after a photograph of West driving to the hoop.

Despite the iconic nature of the West-inspired logo, there have been occasional calls for a modern redesign. West, critics say, is too outdated to represent what the NBA is all about right now, and some younger fans don't even know who he is. But if you really want to symbolize the NBA as it is perceived now, we'd recommend a silhouette of someone altogether different: a corporate-looking, slightly bored fan sitting in a courtside seat.

Chapter 5
HOW AND WHY

Q Why isn't a boxing ring round?

A Boxing has been around for ages because, when you get down to it, humans like to pummel each other. The ancient Greeks were the ones who decided to make it into a legitimate sport: Boxing was introduced as an Olympic event in 688 B.C. The competitors wrapped pieces of soft leather around their hands and proceeded to fight.

The Romans took it a little further, adding bits of metal to the leather. No wonder those guys ruled most of the known world for so long!

Fast forward to England in the eighteenth century. Boxing was popular—and it was violent. The fighters battled each other inside a ring of rope that was lined with—and sometimes held up by—spectators. That's right, a ring. These spectators couldn't be counted on to be sober and often raucously crowded the boxers—the rope ring would get smaller and smaller until the onlookers were practically on top of the fighters. Often the spectators would have a go at it with the boxers themselves.

Understandably, the fighters got a bit testy about the situation. Jack Broughton, a heavyweight champion, came up with a set of rules to protect his fellow boxers in 1743. His plan included a chalked-off square inside which the boxers would fight. Event organizers attached rope to stakes that were pounded into the ground, which prevented the fighting area from changing sizes and from being invaded. Why a square? Because it was easy to make.

Broughton's rules were eventually revised to formalize the square shape. By 1853, the rules stated that matches had to take place in a twenty-four-foot square "ring" that was enclosed by ropes. That, good reader, is the origin of what boxing aficionados call "the squared circle."

Q How come a hockey puck is so hard to follow?

A If you have trouble following a hockey puck as it darts all over the ice, you're probably relatively new to the sport. Spectators who are indoctrinated enough to have lost a tooth or two in the stands—or at their local watering holes—during heated argu-ments about their favorite hockey teams have little trouble tracking that black blur, mostly because they can anticipate the path it will take.

Hockey bills itself as the fastest sport around, and not

just because of the puck. True, in the National Hockey League (NHL), a great scorer's slap shot can easily top 100 miles per hour—in the 1960s, Chicago Blackhawks star Bobby Hull had a slap shot clocked at 120 miles per hour and a wrist shot of 105 miles per hour.

The players themselves are a blur, too. They skate at thirty miles per hour in sprinting situations and at twenty miles per hour when they're cruising down the ice. Such speed is rarely seen in the "foot" team sports, such as football, basketball, and baseball. So the frenetic action around the puck is part of what makes that black disc so hard to follow.

Still, the puck isn't completely innocent in this. Only one inch thick and three inches wide, it's much smaller than a football or basketball.

Hockey fans learn to keep tabs on the puck as they pick up on the nuances of the sport. They anticipate charges down the ice and take notice of how players position themselves for scoring opportunities, and they grow to appreciate the "nonpuck" plays, such as checking and boxing out.

Watching hockey on television can be a challenge, and the Fox network tried to help with its use of the "smart puck" in the mid-1990s. Fox used the wonders of modern technology to transform the puck into a colored dot that had an easy-to-follow trail. The smart puck was widely panned for its distracting effect on the games. The only thing smart about it was that it went into cold storage after Fox's TV contract with the NHL expired. But the smart puck did have some value. It taught us that sometimes harder is better.

Q Why is a checkered flag used in racing?

A The flag-flapping began in October 1906 at the Vanderbilt Cup, a ten-lap, thirty-mile road race through a series of towns on Long Island, New York. As each car crossed the finish line, a black-and-white checkered flag was waved.

The symbolism of the color scheme is open to conjecture: Some say that it is rooted in flags associated with sailing, while others maintain that bicycle racing is a more likely precursor and date the design to a time when men in France wore checkered vests as route markers for bicyclists to follow as they raced through cities.

As interesting as those theories are, the truth most likely can be traced to Sidney Waldon, who worked in public relations for the Packard Motor Car Company at the beginning of the twentieth century. Waldon believed the road-rally races that were popular at the time would benefit from numerous checkpoints, at which race officials would record the times cars arrived and departed. What better way to signify a checkpoint than with a checkered flag?

And so, in July 1906, fifty-four checkpoints were set up along the 1,150-mile AAA/Glidden Tour from Buffalo, New York, to Bretton Woods, New Hampshire. Each checkpoint was marked with a thirty-two-by-thirty-two-inch flag that had four checkered rows.

Over twelve days, each car on the tour raced from checkpoint to checkpoint. At each of these stations, a checkered flag prompted drivers to stop so that their times could be recorded and their cars could be inspected.

The concept of a checkered flag so impressed race committee member Willie K. Vanderbilt that he brought it to his race, the aforementioned Vanderbilt Cup. From there, the checkered flag assumed its place in racing history.

Q Why do golfers hate to putt?

A Most golfers hate to putt, at some level. Sometimes at a very visible, sweaty level. Even though golfers know it's possible to screw up every single shot from tee to green, putting is what winds up freaking them out.

Why? The easy answer is that putting is hard. Even for the pros. "I play along every year waiting for one week, maybe two, when I can putt," says Larry Nelson. And Nelson has been one of the best putters in professional golf for almost three decades.

We amateurs tend to think that pros make almost all of their putts. In fact, they miss at least six out of every hundred from two feet—an astonishingly high number. They make no more than one in every six putts from twenty feet. All we do is make things worse by imagining it's easier for the pros than it is.

And this gets us closer to the heart of the matter. Golfers tend to think too much, especially on the green.

"*Happy Gilmore* is a pretty good instructional film," says PGA teaching pro Peter Donahue. He explains that the loopy Adam Sandler character has the most vital trait in a good putter: He's happy to putt. "Golfers train themselves not to love to shoot but to be afraid to miss," Donahue says. "It's like Red Auerbach said in basketball: 'I don't care if you miss, just don't be afraid to shoot.'"

The best putters in the world are touring and teaching pros, obviously. But the next best, according to Donahue, are beginners. Why? It goes back to that thinking thing. Beginners don't ponder—they just putt.

After searching far and wide, we did uncover at least one person who likes to putt: PGA golfer Ben Crenshaw. "From the very beginning I enjoyed putting," he says in his autobiography. "I loved putting because it was just plain fun, and it fascinated me to watch the ball roll over those blades of grass."

Crenshaw, of course, is in the minority. Take it from Larry Eimers, a sports psychologist from Durham, North Carolina, who has counseled many a tortured putter: "You're in a risk area where you're liable to suffer humiliation or embarrassment if you miss it. ...Everyone hates [the short] putt, because if you make it, no one gives a damn, but if you miss it, everyone raises their eyebrows. In the end, you're working eighteen holes to avoid humiliation."

Did we mention that golfers hate to putt?

Q How come nobody else calls it soccer?

 Millions of kids across the United States grow up playing a game that their parents hardly know, a game that virtually everyone else in the world calls football. It's soccer to us, of course, and although Americans might be ridiculed for calling it this, the corruption is actually British in origin.

Soccer—football, as the Brits and billions of others insist—has an ancient history. Evidence of games resembling soccer has been found in cultures that date to the third century B.C. The Greeks had a version that they called *episkyro*. The Romans brought their version of the sport along when they colonized what is now England and Ireland. Over the next millennium, the game evolved into a free-wheeling, roughneck competition—matches often involved kicking, shoving, and punching.

In England and Ireland, the sport was referred to as football; local and regional rules varied widely. Two different games—soccer and rugby—slowly emerged from this disorganized mess. The Football Association was formed in 1863 to standardize the rules of soccer and to separate it from rugby. The term "soccer" most likely is derived from Association's work.

During the late nineteenth century, the Brits developed the linguistic habit of shortening words and adding "ers" or "er." (We suffer this quirk to this day in expressions like "preggers." A red card to the Brits on this one.) One popular theory holds that given the trend, it was natural that those playing "Assoc." football were playing "assoccers" or "soccer." The term died out in England, but was revived in the United States in the early part of the twentieth century to separate the imported sport with the round white ball from the American sport with the oblong brown ball.

Q Why is soccer popular everywhere except the United States?

A Every four years, there's a sporting event that transfixes almost the entire globe. In hundreds of countries, parades are held, commerce and transportation slow to a crawl, and the home team's chances are the topic of nearly every discussion. No, it's not the Olympics—it's the World Cup. And it's only in very recent years that Americans have paid any attention.

Even though playing youth soccer is a veritable rite of passage in the United States, it seems that most Americans lose interest in the sport somewhere around age twelve. It's not as if adult soccer doesn't exist in this country—there's even a professional soccer league, known as Major League Soccer, which enjoys a degree of popularity and respect that's on a level with the Professional Miniature Golf Association. Yet in the rest of the world, soccer inspires passion and rabidity. The United States' indifference to soccer has baffled sports journalists and analysts for decades. Here are a few theories:

• We don't like games in which you can't use your hands. Some observers have pointed out that the myth of America is largely constructed upon the idea of the self-made, hardworking man. A man who uses his hands to build houses with hand-cut logs and hand-laid bricks, who uses his hands to plow the earth and bake his bread. That none of this has happened for a hundred and fifty years makes little difference to this theory's proponents.

• We don't like games without action or scoring. Soccer seems pretty boring, especially to the uninitiated. A lot of kicking the ball across a field, with very little effort being made to advance to the other team's goal. Games often end in ties or with a total tally of fewer than three goals. Yes, watching soccer for a few hours can be pretty deadening.

• We don't like the players' antics. Have you ever watched a soccer game? Two-thirds of it consists of players flopping lamely or gesticulating wildly when they get called for a penalty. We Americans are stand-up guys, always behaving courteously, willing to take the blame when it's our fault and the first to admit we're wrong when we're wrong. Okay, maybe not so much—as evidenced by the steroids scandal in baseball.

The most likely reason Americans don't like soccer is that, quite frankly, we suck at it. America has a big ego, and getting crushed in soccer by countries like Colombia and Costa Rica doesn't do much to inflate it.

The problem, though, is that if we don't pay attention to the sport, we'll probably never field a team that's good enough to be consistently competitive on the international stage. This will further suppress national interest, triggering a vicious cycle that will likely keep soccer down—unless an American Pelé or Diego Maradona comes along to bring it to the forefront of the country's consciousness.

In the meantime, sports analysts will continue to puzzle over why Americans don't care about soccer. It's kind of like another vexing sports question: Why do Americans watch NASCAR?

Q Why do baseball fans stretch in the seventh inning?

A Presidents of the United States have long had a connection to America's national pastime. Ronald Reagan famously recreated the play-by-play of Chicago Cubs games without watching any of the action (preparing him quite nicely, some say, for his presidency). George W. Bush was part-owner of the Texas Rangers for nearly a decade, becoming a managing partner thanks to his oil-company pals (preparing him quite nicely, some say, for his presidency). And Opening Day wouldn't be complete without the sitting president awkwardly throwing out the first pitch, a tradition started in 1910 by William Howard Taft (for more details on that tradition, see page 127).

According to baseball folklore—of which there is a seemingly endless amount—it was the portly, peace-loving Taft who also started the tradition of the seventh-inning stretch at that same Opening Day game in 1910. As the tale goes, Taft, who was a baseball fanatic (and a promising catcher before embarking upon a political career), rose to stretch his corpulent frame after the top of the seventh inning. The crowd, believing Taft was departing, rose in respect for its commander-in-chief, only to somewhat confusedly sit back down when Taft returned to his seat as the bottom of the inning commenced. Thus, the seventh-inning stretch was born.

Like many apocryphal tales, the story of Taft inventing the seventh-inning stretch is dubious. Indeed, the practice of fans stretching in the middle of the seventh inning goes back to at least 1869. In that year, Harry Wright, the manager of the Cincinnati Red Stockings, wrote a letter to a friend in which he claimed "the spectators all arise between halves of the seventh inning, extend their legs and arms." That sounds suspiciously like a stretch, doesn't it? There is no record as to why this tradition existed, though the hard wooden benches of the grandstand might provide a cogent explanation.

Nowadays, the seventh-inning stretch is entrenched in baseball tradition and often features the crowd singing along to the traditional "Take Me Out to the Ball Game" (or in polka-loving Milwaukee, "Roll Out the Barrel"). Of course, with the modern trend of baseball stadiums cutting off alcohol sales after the seventh inning, the seventh-inning stretch has turned into more of a seventh-inning sprint—to the beer stand.

Q In soccer, why are yellow cards yellow and red cards red?

A Considering that soccer has existed in its modern form since the mid-nineteenth century, it's rather strange that no formal penalty system—i.e., red cards and yellow cards—was put into place until the latter part of the twentieth century.

The situation is stranger still when you consider the innocuous way in which red cards and yellow cards came to be. Ken Aston, a headmaster at a British school, was sitting at a stoplight after attending a World Cup quarterfinal between England and Argentina in 1966 when an idea that would change soccer popped into his head. "As I drove down Kensington High Street, the traffic light turned red," Aston said. "I thought, 'Yellow, take it easy; red, stop, you're off.'"

Aston's brainstorm was prompted by the lack of formal, announced penalties in soccer at the time. As ridiculous as it seems, players could be penalized in a soccer match or ejected without any sort of declaration from the referee. In the England versus Argentina match, numerous players had been ejected by the referee without being told of their infraction. Aston knew the obvious: Soccer needed a formalized way to keep players and fans informed of infractions.

The global soccer community embraced Aston's idea. The system of yellow and red cards was adopted in time for the 1970 World Cup in Mexico City. For those who don't follow soccer closely, here is a quick tutorial on why a ref would pull out a yellow card or red card.

A yellow card is presented to a player as a warning after any of the following infractions:

- Unsportsmanlike conduct
- Dissent by word or actions
- Persistent rule-breaking
- Delaying the restart of play
- Defending a corner kick or free kick too closely
- Entering or leaving the field without referee permission

A red card is given if a player receives two yellow cards in a match, or when any of the following occurs:

- Serious foul play
- Violence
- Spitting
- Denying an obvious goal-scoring opportunity by deliberately handling the ball
- Fouling an opponent to prevent an obvious goal-scoring opportunity
- Offensive or threatening language

If shown a red card, a player is "sent off" and cannot be replaced, forcing his or her team to compete one player short.

Since Aston's epiphany, the practice of issuing colored cards has been adopted by other sports besides soccer, including volleyball, rugby, field hockey, lacrosse, and handball. In rugby, a yellow card gets you sent to the "sin bin," which is like the penalty box in hockey.

In soccer, a yellow gets you a break from the game. It sounds genteel enough, just as Aston imagined it while idling at that traffic light. The reality, however, has been something different, especially in soccer-crazed Europe. Sometimes an ill-issued yellow card can spark a near-riot, which begs the question: Why doesn't soccer have a "sin bin," too…for its hooligan fans?

Q Why do you have to be quiet when a golfer is swinging?

A At first blush, the answer seems obvious: So the golfer can concentrate. But it brings up interesting subsequent questions: Why do golfers insist that they be allowed to concentrate when, say, football and baseball players do not? The answers have to do with the particular demands of golf and the particular social milieu in which it's been played for several centuries.

Let's start with the physical and mental demands. There is probably no other sport that requires such a combination of power and precision—of power applied precisely. Tiger Woods propels a full drive at about 150 miles per hour, yet he's envisioning a landing area that's not much more than ten yards wide, some 240 yards down the fairway.

If one part of Woods's body moves more than a fraction of an inch in the wrong way while he swings, or if the timing of his swing is imprecise—he releases his wrists a fraction of a second too soon, say—the ball can travel thirty, forty, fifty yards or more off-target.

It's just as demanding on the green. Two hundred years ago, golf greens were as shaggy as a carpet. Now, the better the course, the shorter the greens are. At Augusta National Golf Club during the Masters Tournament, they are just a little more forgiving than linoleum. The golfer needs to control every nuance of the length, speed, and pace of his putting swing in order to prevent the ball from scurrying yards past the hole. This—like his drive—requires fantastic physical coordination, sensory sophistication, and concentration.

But not too much concentration. The hallmark of a hack golfer is his reliance on a mental checklist before every swing. "Head down, shoulder tucked, left arm straight..." More experienced golfers have drilled these requisites into their unconscious mind—and into their muscles.

But in order for that natural process to take place as programmed—in order to achieve the right combination of concentration and calm—they need quiet. Tiger Woods is so routinized, in fact, that he loses his temper when fans make unexpected noises or take pictures during his swing.

Maybe if golfers grew up amid bedlam, like football players do, they wouldn't mind the distractions. But they're accustomed to quiet. Which gets to the matter of tradition. For much of its history, golf has been a club sport. Clubs are laden with rules that seem arbitrary and stuffy to outsiders but make the social experience more meaningful for members. There are all sorts of formalities in golf clubs regarding gentlemanly behavior and the like, and these have extended to the course, where golfers go out of their way to observe them.

For example, the player who had the lowest score on the previous hole always tees off first on the next. If someone forgets and accidentally tees off out of turn, it's embarrassing, even among good friends. This powerful social component of golf colors every minute on the course, and keeping quiet during a golfer's swing is the most obligatory courtesy. So you see, as with almost everything in golf, there's more to this custom than meets the eyes . . .and ears.

Why does K stand for strikeout?

A To the uninitiated, a baseball scorecard can look like a set of hieroglyphs in need of the Rosetta stone: numbers, circles, lines, colored diamonds, and more abbreviations than an IM conversation between hyperactive teens. And when the seven-dollar beers start flowing in the grandstand—forget about it.

Actually, most of these abbreviations are fairly easy to decipher. It doesn't take a sabermetrician to figure out that HR stands for "home run" and BB stands for "base on balls." But what genius designated K the symbol for "strikeout"?

That would be Henry Chadwick—writer, National Baseball Hall of Fame member, and inventor of the baseball box score. Chadwick was born in England in 1824 and grew up as an avid fan of the English ball games cricket and rounders. He emigrated to the United States as a young man, and in the 1850s, as the relatively new sport of baseball gained popularity in America, Chadwick became a devoted fan. Chadwick was a newspaper reporter in New York at the time, and at his suggestion, the city's major newspapers began to include coverage of baseball games to their agendas.

A lot happens in a baseball game, and Chadwick knew that it wasn't always easy to keep track of what was going on—especially when the thirteen-cent beers started flowing in the grandstand. In 1861, in a treatise curiously titled *Beadle's Dime Base-Ball Player*, Chadwick introduced a scorecard for baseball games. It was adapted from one used by reporters to keep track of cricket matches.

Chadwick's early scorecard was an unwieldy spreadsheet worthy of Excel. It involved twenty-nine columns that were thirteen rows deep, and provided space for stats of the day like "bounds" and "muffs." It also included space to record what happened on a play-to-play basis, which helped writers recreate the game in the following day's newspaper.

Because S was so common in baseball's statistical lexicon ("stolen base," "sacrifice," "strikeout"), Chadwick chose K to represent the whiff. Why K? It's the last letter in "struck," which was the common term that was used to describe the strikeout in the 1860s.

The baseball scorecard has grown more comprehensible over the years, but much of Chadwick's original form and symbolism survives, including the use of K for a strikeout. Nowadays, many fans take it further by using a normal K to represent a swinging strikeout and a backward K to represent a called third strike.

Chadwick, who devoted his life to promoting baseball, would no doubt delight at the immense popularity the game has attained. It's doubtful that he'd be impressed by the beer sales, however: Chadwick was a strong supporter of the temperance movement.

Q What's up with the scoring system in tennis?

A The British are an odd bunch. They call trucks "lorries," drugstores "chemists," and telephones "blowers." They put meat in pies, celebrate a holiday called Boxing Day that has nothing to do with boxing, and eat something

called "spotted dick." So it shouldn't be surprising that tennis, one of Britain's national pastimes, has such a bizarre scoring system.

For those who haven't been to the tennis club lately, here's a refresher on how scoring works. The first player to achieve four points is the winner of the match, but points are not counted by one, two, six, or any other logical number—they go by fifteen for the first two points of the game, then ten for the third point. The sequence, then, is: 0–15–30–40. Except it's not zero—it's called "love." So: love–15–30–40. To confuse matters further, if both players are tied at forty, it's called "deuce." Just trying to figure out this scoring system makes one long for a gin gimlet and a cold compress.

Gin gimlets, in fact, may have been the order of the day when modern tennis was invented. According to most tennis historians, it dates back to the early 1870s, when the delightfully named Major Walter Clopton Wingfield devised a lawn game for the entertainment of party guests on his English country estate. Wingfield (whose bust graces the Wimbledon Tennis Museum) based his game on an older form of tennis that long had been popular in France and England, called "real tennis."

Unfortunately, the origin of tennis' odd scoring system is as obfuscated as the system itself. A number of historians argue that Wingfield, being somewhat of a pompous ass, borrowed the terms for his new game from the older French version, even though they made no sense once adapted into English. Hence, *l'oeuf* (meaning "egg") turned into "love." And *à deux le jeu* ("to two the game") transformed into "deuce."

Furthermore, Wingfield opted to borrow the counting system from earlier versions of tennis—in French, scoring mimicked the quarter-hours of the clock: 15–30–45. For some unknown reason (possibly too many gin gimlets), 45 became 40, and we have the scoring system that we know and love (no pun intended) today.

There are plenty of other theories about where the scoring system originated, including "love" coming from the Flemish *lof* (meaning "honor") and "deuce" originating in ancient card games. Others argue that scoring by fifteen was based on the value of the sou, a medieval French coin. However, in the absence of definitive evidence, we attribute the ludicrous scoring system to drunken Brits.

Q Why do the Dallas Cowboys and Detroit Lions always play on Thanksgiving?

A You could call it a tradition that's as American as apple pie, except that it happens on the one day of the year that apple is trumped by a different flavor of pie.

Despite the fact that few people have any interest in ever seeing the Detroit Lions play, and because most people love to hate the Dallas Cowboys (no Thanksgiving feast is complete without at least a dash of animosity), millions of Americans look forward to that one special Thursday in November when they can do what they usually get to do only on Sundays: eat too much and watch a lot of professional football. The games are as much a part of Thanksgiving as turkey and stuffing.

But the truth is, Americans used to get a lot more football on Thanksgiving than they do now. As many as six games were played on a single Thanksgiving during the 1920s; of course, television was not yet even a glint in the nation's eye, so hardly anyone saw them. Just as the holiday football tradition began to wane, the Chicago Bears rolled into Detroit for a 1934 Thanksgiving showdown. The Bears were the defending NFL champions and had an 11–0 record; the Lions were 10–1.

The Western Division championship was on the line, but the Lions were new to Detroit that year and attendance had lagged—the largest crowd of the season had been about fifteen thousand. Therefore, Lions owner George A. "Dick" Richards took notice when twenty-six thousand people showed up on Thanksgiving for a game that was broadcast nationally on NBC radio. Richards made sure the Lions played host to the Bears on Thanksgiving for the next four years, and a national event was born.

The tradition took a hiatus during World War II, but the Lions picked it up again in 1945, and they have played on every Thanksgiving since. During the 1950s, when football and television began their torrid romance, the Lions were in their heyday and had nationwide appeal. They hosted the Green Bay Packers every Thanksgiving from 1951 to 1963. It was usually the only game of the day, until the upstart American Football League began staging its own Turkey Day matchup in 1960.

In 1966, the NFL decided to counter by boosting its holiday offering to two games, and Cowboys president and general manager Tex Schramm was quick to seize the opportunity. "I was very aware of the impact of television," Schramm said. "What does everybody do after they eat turkey? They sit and watch TV." As the Lions descended into mediocrity, Dallas became known as "America's Team."

But traditions die hard, so the Lions continue to serve up our national appetizer each Thanksgiving. Shortly thereafter, the Cowboys deliver the main course. (There have been two exceptions to this rule: The St. Louis Cardinals replaced the Cowboys as hosts in both1975 and 1977.)

The tradition has, in fact, evolved somewhat. In 2006, the NFL added a night game that is intended to function as our national dessert—for those hardy souls who manage to remain conscious into the evening.

Q Why do college football coaches have armed state troopers with them on the sideline?

A A couple of state troopers are the ultimate accessories for a major-college football coach, especially in the pigskin-crazed South. No one is certain how the tradition started, but it's usually attributed to Paul "Bear" Bryant, who was a legendary coach at the University of Alabama. The story is that Bear got a trooper entourage for security in 1958 or 1959. Not to be outdone, Ralph "Shug" Jordan, coach at Auburn University, Alabama's bitter in-state rival, secured a larger posse of troopers soon after. Let the games begin.

The tradition is both ceremonial and practical. Ceremonially, the troopers represent state pride, whether at home or away. Troopers have no law enforcement authority in another state, but armed and dressed in their official garb, they can be an imposing presence on the sideline.

From a practical perspective, the troopers' chief responsibility is to provide protection. This rarely is an issue during the game, but the playing field can fill up quickly with excited and rambunctious fans once the final seconds have ticked away. It is the job of troopers to escort the coach through the chaos to midfield for the traditional handshake with the opposing coach (who also might be flanked by troopers) and then to the locker room.

This sort of security doesn't come cheap. In 2008, ten schools in Alabama each paid the state police more than thirty-eight thousand dollars for "football detail." Some troopers in other states provide coach protection at no cost, as long as the college pays for meals and travel expenses.

The practice is nearly ubiquitous among NCAA Division I-A teams in the Southeastern Conference and has also caught on with some schools in the ACC, Big East, Big 12, and Big Ten conferences. Trooper detail hasn't taken root in the West, however—the Pacific-10 Conference is explicitly opposed to the practice. Teams without trooper support generally rely on campus police for coach security.

For a trooper assigned to a coach, staying calm, cool, and collected might be the toughest part of the gig. Troopers typically are huge fans of their assigned teams, but they're expected to maintain stoic professionalism. And this is no small feat if they've just witnessed a game-winning touchdown.

Q Why is a round of golf eighteen holes?

 It's been suggested that a round of golf is eighteen holes because there are eighteen shots in a bottle of Scotch whisky. This theory is sexy—and even has an element of logic—but it's not true. A fifth of Scotch is about twenty-six ounces, and if you break that into eighteen shots, you'll have some abnormally large belts of booze.

No, the answer is as simple as this: There are eighteen holes in an official round of golf because the Royal and Ancient Golf Club of St. Andrews in Scotland told its members so in 1858.

This is just one of the ways that the spiritual home of golf has influenced the game we play today. Now, we're not saying the R&A stated that every official round of golf had to be eighteen holes—it only stipulated that this was the case on its course. But since we're talking St. Andrews, one of the courses on which the British Open is played, and because the R&A has been so influential in other respects, the formality caught on.

There's nothing intrinsically right about eighteen holes—it's just what St. Andrews' members tended to play. For much of the club's history, the course didn't even have eighteen distinct holes. Until 1764, St. Andrews had twelve holes, most of which ran along the water, "links" style. Members played them in order, then played ten of them backward, for a round of twenty-two.

That year, members decided to shorten a round to eighteen holes. It took nearly a hundred years for the club to standardize this as an official round, though its members continued to play rounds of various lengths for their own fun. In 1867, nine years after St. Andrews made eighteen official, Carnoustie Golf Links (another legendary course in Scotland) added eight holes to make eighteen. The trend had begun.

Before all this, courses came in every configuration imaginable, usually featuring between a few and a dozen holes. Golf had not yet become the ritualized game that it is today, so players didn't feel compelled to play a specific number of holes.

Curiously, there is a trend developing today toward returning to less-formalized play. A round of eighteen holes was fine for well-heeled members of the R&A, as well as for American dads in the 1950s through the 1980s, who felt entitled to a full Saturday at the golf course after a hard week at the office. But today's dads are schlepping the kids to soccer on Saturdays while overworked moms get a break, and golf courses have had to improvise. Some now offer "6 after 6"—six holes of golf and a burger after 6:00 P.M.—just to get folks out to play. It's possible that someday eighteen holes will seem as antiquated as St. Andrews' original twelve do to us now.

Q Why does the umpire turn his backside toward the pitcher when sweeping off home plate?

A Umpires love decorum—and why not? When your job is to keep a bunch of adrenaline-fueled jocks in line, that's perfectly understandable.

In its section on cleaning home plate, the American Legion Umpires National Tournament Manual begins, rather pompously, with this statement: "Every gesture and motion of an umpire means something." The manual then instructs the home plate umpire to turn his back to the pitcher's mound before bending over, "as a courtesy to fans." Hey, if an ump's every gesture means something, what's the pitcher supposed to make of being mooned every inning?

There's no consensus on the exact reason that umpires clean the plate this way. Some "experts" claim that it lets the players know beyond a shadow of a doubt that time has been called. Others say that it protects the ump if a pitch gets thrown at him by mistake while he's doing the dusting. (It's better to get hit in the butt than in the head.)

As the American Legion manual suggests, it may simply be a display of courtesy to the fans. But that doesn't stop umpires from using the move for other purposes, like surreptitiously lecturing an argumentative batter or catcher. It's a way to get a point across without showing anybody up.

Not all umpires are so formal when it comes to cleaning the plate. Former big-league ump Ken Kaiser found that he could get the job done with a quick swipe of his foot. Kaiser was amused to learn that this irritated some of his more tradition-bound colleagues. "I didn't grow up expecting to hear the commissioner of baseball telling me to clean my plate," Kaiser explained in his book *Planet of the Umps*. "As long as I could see the plate, it was clean enough for me."

Why is there a dropped-third-strike rule in baseball?

On the surface, baseball is pretty simple. In the memorable words of former major-league manager Lee Elia: "The name of the game is hit the ball, catch the ball, and get the [bleeping] job done." But getting the [bleeping] job done and maintaining that apparent simplicity requires a few rules for resolving unusual situations—for example, the infield fly and the balk—that most fans know about without ever fully understanding.

Such is the case with the dropped-third-strike rule (or, more accurately, the uncaught-third-strike rule). The philosophy behind the rule is based on common sense: A team in the field shouldn't be given credit for an out if it screws up at the end of the play. On a third strike, if the catcher drops the pitch, or if the pitch bounds away from the catcher, it's equivalent to any other fielder dropping a fly ball. The batter is free to try to reach first base, and the defense has to be more proactive to record the out, by either tagging the batter or throwing him out at first base.

Without some modifications, the dropped-third-strike rule would offer the defense an unfair advantage. This is where the rule gets a little confusing. Say there's a runner on first and no outs—on a third strike, the catcher could purposely drop the ball, obliging the batter to run to first, which would in turn oblige the runner on first to make a break for second. With the batter and runner caught off-guard, the catcher could pick up the ball and initiate an easy double play by throwing to second for the force-out, followed by a quick throw from second to first to retire the now-running batter.

To eliminate the possibility of this sort of chicanery, the dropped-third-strike rule only applies under the following conditions: when there are two outs and a double play is pointless, or when first base is open with fewer than two outs so there is no chance for a force-out. With fewer than two outs and first base occupied, the batter is out on strike three regardless of whether the catcher catches the pitch.

The infield fly rule is also designed to eliminate similarly cheap double (or triple) plays initiated by intentional errors with runners on base. Now, if you want to figure out the [bleeping] balk rule, you'll have to go to another [bleeping] place.

Q Why is a marathon 26.2 miles?

A To most of us, running a marathon is incomprehensible. Driving 26.2 miles is perhaps a possibility, though only if we stop at least once for Fritos. Equally incomprehensible is the number itself, 26.2. Why isn't a marathon 26.4 miles? Or 25.9? Why, oh why, is the magic number 26.2?

To answer this curious question, we must examine the history of the marathon. Our current marathon is descended from a legend about the most famous runner in ancient Greece, a soldier named Philippides (his name was later corrupted in text to Pheidippides). For much of the fifth century B.C., the Greeks were at odds with the neighboring Persian Empire; in 490 B.C., the mighty Persians, led by Darius I, attacked the Greeks at the city of Marathon. Despite being badly outnumbered, the Greeks managed to fend off the Persian troops (and ended Darius's attempts at conquering Greece).

After the victory, the legend holds, Philippides ran in full armor from Marathon to Athens—about twenty-five miles—to announce the good news. After several hours of running through the rugged Greek countryside, he arrived at the gates of Athens crying, "Rejoice, we conquer!" as Athenians rejoiced. Philippides then fell over dead. Despite a great deal of debate about the accuracy of this story, the legend still held such sway in the Greek popular mind that when the modern Olympic Games were revived in Athens in 1896, a long-distance running event known as a "marathon" was instituted.

How did the official marathon distance get to be 26.2 miles if the journey of Philippides was about twenty-five? Well, in the first two Olympic Games, something closer to the "Philippides distance" was indeed used. The first Olympic Marathon was 24.85 miles (40,000 meters) in length. (For the record, the winner was Greek postal worker Spiridon Louis, who completed the course in 2 hours, 58 minutes, 50 seconds, with an average pace of 7.11 minutes per mile.)

But things changed in 1908, when the Olympic Games were held in London. The British Olympic committee determined that the marathon route would start at Windsor Castle and end in front of the royal box in front of London's newly built Olympic Stadium, a distance that happened to measure 26 miles, 385 yards.

There was no good reason for the whims of British lords to become the standard, but 26.2 somehow got ingrained in the sporting psyche. By the 1924 Olympics in Paris, this arbitrary distance had become the standard for all marathons.

Today, winning a marathon—heck, even completing one—is considered a premier athletic accomplishment. In cities such as Boston, New York, and Chicago, thousands of professionals and amateurs turn out to participate. Of course, wiser people remember what happened to Philippides when he foolishly tried to run such a long distance. Pass the Fritos.

Q Why do marathon runners wrap themselves in foil after a race?

A While we're speaking of modern marathons, here's another question. Watching thousands of marathon runners clog the streets of a major city is odd. Odder still is the sight of these runners huddled in foil wrappers after the race. What are those things anyway?

After suffering through 26.2 miles of agony on the pavement, it seems that the last thing you would need is someone packaging you up like you're about to be sold off of a downtown food cart. But in fact, you cover a runner in foil for the same reason you would a baked potato or a burrito—to keep in heat.

These foil coverings are called HeatSheets, and they can be lifesavers for people who run marathons, particularly during cold weather. Runners shed clothing as they move through a long-distance race, usually finishing in shorts and a T-shirt. The body heats up during a race and, therefore, sweats as a cooling mechanism. It's virtually impossible for a runner to drink enough liquid during a race to offset the moisture he or she loses through sweating, so dehydration sets in. This also prevents the body from cooling properly.

That's not a huge problem until the end of the race, when a runner begins to cool down—rapidly, if the weather is chilly. The cool-down can happen so quickly that it fools the body's internal sensors, which haven't gotten the message that the race is over and continue to shed heat. In such a case, dehydration quickly turns to hypothermia.

HeatSheets prevent the rapid loss of body heat. They're made of Mylar (a plastic sheeting) and coated with a thin layer of aluminum, which keeps heat trapped against the body. In addition, because of their economical size, HeatSheets are better to hand out after a race than, say, blankets or sweatshirts.

They just look a lot sillier.

Chapter 6
HOW IT ALL GOT STARTED

Q **What were baseball's predecessors?**

A Baseball didn't spring out of nowhere, nor was it invented by a single person. Games involving sticks and balls go back thousands of years. They've been traced to the Mayans in the Western Hemisphere and to Egypt at the time of the Pharaohs. There are historical references to Greeks, Chinese, and Vikings "playing ball." And a woodcut from 14th-century France shows what seem to be a batter, pitcher, and fielders.

By the 18th century, references to "baseball" were appearing in British publications. In an 1801 book entitled *The Sports and Pastimes of the People of England*, Joseph Strutt claimed that baseball-like games could be traced back to the 14th century and that baseball was a descendant of a British game called "stoolball." The earliest known reference to stoolball is in a 1330 poem by William Pagula, who recommended to priests that the game be forbidden within the nation's churchyards.

In stoolball (which is still played in England, mostly by women), a batter stands before a target, perhaps an upturned stool, while another player pitches a ball to the batter. If the batter hits the ball (with a bat or his/her hand) and it is caught by a fielder, the batter is out. Ditto if the pitched ball hits a stool leg.

It seems that stoolball eventually split into two different styles. One became English "base-ball," which turned into "rounders" in England but evolved into "town ball" when it reached the United States. The other side of stoolball turned into cricket. From town ball came the two styles that dominated baseball's development: the Massachusetts Game and the New York Game. The former had no foul or fair territory; runners were put out by being hit with a thrown ball when off the base ("soaking"), and as soon as one out was made, the offense and defense switched sides. The latter established the concept of foul lines, and each team was given three "outs" to an inning. Perhaps more significantly, soaking was eliminated in favor of the more gentlemanly tag. The two versions coexisted in the first three decades of the 19th century, but when the Manhattanites codified their rules in 1845, it became easier for more and more groups to play the New York style.

A book printed in France in 1810 laid out the rules for a bat/base/running game called "poison ball," in which there were two teams of eight to ten players, four bases (one called "home"), a pitcher, a batter, and flyball outs. Different variations of the game went by different names: "Tip-cat" and "trap ball" were notable for how important the bat had become. It was no longer used merely to avoid hurting one's hand; it had become a real cudgel, to swat the ball a long way.

In the early 1840s, Alexander Cartwright, a New York City engineer, was one of a group who met regularly to play baseball, and he may have been the mastermind behind organizing, formalizing, and writing down the rules of the game. The group called themselves The Knickerbocker Club, and their constitution, enacted on September 23, 1845, led the way for the game we know today.

You may have heard the myth that a man named Abner Doubleday (a Civil War general on the Union side) founded the game. But even though the origins of baseball are murky, there's one thing we know for sure: Abner Doubleday had nothing to do with it. The Mills Commission was organized in 1905 by Albert Spalding to search for a definitive American source for baseball. They "found" it in an ambiguous letter spun by a Cooperstown resident (who turned out to be crazy). But Doubleday wasn't even in Cooperstown when the author of the letter said he had invented the game. Also, "The Boy's Own Book" presented the rules for a baseball-like game ten years before Doubleday's alleged "invention."

Q How did Adidas, Nike, and Reebok get their names?

A Sportswear giants Adidas and Puma were both founded in the late 1940s, and both are headquartered in the town of Herzogenaurach, Germany. Is it just a coincidence that a town of about 22,000 people hosts two international companies? Nope—the companies were founded by feuding brothers, and Herzogenaurach was their hometown.

In the 1920s, brothers Adolf and Rudolph Dassler owned a shoe company together. The Dassler company became known for its athletic shoes and was given a boost to their reputation when they supplied shoes to Jesse Owens in the 1936 Olympic Games. However, eventually there was conflict between the brothers, and they split apart. In 1948, Adolf "Adi" Dassler founded Adidas

AG, using three letters from his nickname and three letters from his last name. In the same time period, Rudolph set up a competing company that was originally called Ruda. However, it shortly became Puma (officially, Puma Schuhfabrick Rudolf Dassler).

The brothers did not reconcile before death, and the rivalry between the two companies continues—especially in the town of Herzogenaurach, where what you're wearing on your feet is a very serious matter.

A subsidiary of Adidas since 2005, Reebok was established in 1895 in Britain under the name J.W. Foster and Sons. In 1958, J.W. Foster's grandsons Joe and Jeff Foster decided to rename the company. They chose "reebok," the name of an African gazelle. The American spelling would be rhebok, but the Fosters were using a South African dictionary, which had the alternate spelling. (Another alternate spelling is ribbok, if any other companies are looking for a brand name...)

In 1964, Blue Ribbon Sports was founded in Beaverton, Oregon. In 1971, its founders went searching for a catchy, energetic company name. Designer Jeff Johnson suggested Nike, the name of the Greek goddess of victory. The now-famous "swoosh" was first used in the same year.

The iconic "Just do it" came a little later. When ad exec Dan Wieden met with a group of Nike employees to talk about a new ad campaign, he told them, "You Nike guys...you just do it." The result was one of the most effective taglines in advertising history. During the first ten years of this award-winning campaign, Nike's percent of the sport shoe market shot up from 18 to 43 percent.

Still headquartered in Oregon, Nike is now the largest sportswear manufacturer in the world.

Q Which president was the first to throw out the first pitch at a baseball game?

A On April 14, 1910, President William Howard Taft decided on a whim to attend the Senators' Opening Day game against the Philadelphia A's, showing up unannounced at National Park. Umpire Billy Evans noticed President Taft sitting in the stands and asked him if he would throw out the first ball, something that was usually done by a local politician. Taft's toss began a tradition of first pitches that has been carried out by every American president since then, with the exception of Jimmy Carter.

Presidential first pitches have featured dramatic and comedic high-lights—and lowlights. Following are some of the more memorable first pitch moments.

William H. Taft: When making his trendsetting first pitch in 1910, Taft had a Hall of Fame partner. Washington Senators ace Walter Johnson, normally on the pitching end of the baseball battery, received Taft's historic throw. President Taft gave Johnson the ball the next day with the following inscription: "To Walter Johnson with hope that he may continue to be as formidable as in yesterday's game. William H. Taft."

Two years later, Taft missed the opener in Washington while tending to the aftermath of the Titanic disaster. Vice President James Sherman filled in for Taft, throwing out the first pitch on April 19 before a scant crowd of just over 10,000 fans.

Woodrow Wilson: He ventured out of the nation's capital to become the first president to attend a World Series game. On October 9, 1915, Wilson threw out the first pitch at Philadelphia's Baker Bowl, moments before Game 2 of the Series matchup between the Boston Red Sox and the Philadelphia Phillies.

Franklin Delano Roosevelt:
A true fan of the game, FDR holds the record for most Opening Day first pitches (eight) and overall first pitches (11). In FDR's case, practice didn't make perfect: At the 1940 opener in Washington, Roosevelt made an errant toss, breaking the camera of an unfortunate photographer from the *Washington Post.*

Harry Truman: Due to World War II, Roosevelt refrained from visiting major-league ballparks in 1942, '43, and '44. Truman ended the presidential drought when he threw out the first pitch before a game on September 8, 1945, between the Senators and the St. Louis Browns. Truman's return to the ballpark signaled that baseball, depleted because of players' involvement in military service, was now back to full strength.

John F. Kennedy: An avid fan of the Boston Red Sox, JFK stayed to watch every inning of the four games he attended while in office. As president, he threw out the first pitch at the newly built D.C. Stadium in 1962. The stadium was later renamed in honor of Kennedy's brother Robert.

Richard Nixon: Arguably the most knowledgeable baseball fan of all American presidents, Nixon took part in a unique first pitch ceremony on April 6, 1973. A POW named Major Luna and Nixon, participating in his first ceremonial toss away from the city of Washington, both threw out first pitches before the game at Anaheim Stadium in California. According to Dick Young of the New York Daily News, Nixon was not just "a guy that shows up at season openers to take bows and get his picture in the paper and has to have his secretary of state tell him where first base is. This man knows baseball."

Gerald Ford: At the 1976 All-Star Game, the athletic president thrilled fans by doing double duty: throwing out one pitch right-handed to Johnny Bench of the Cincinnati Reds and a second pitch left-handed to Carlton Fisk of the Boston Red Sox.

Jimmy Carter: Carter once told Commissioner Bowie Kuhn that he preferred playing sports to watching them, which explains why he attended only one major-league game while in office—the seventh game of the 1979 World Series between the Orioles and the Pirates. Carter chose not to throw out the first pitch on that occasion, and he remains the only president since Taft who has not thrown one.

Ronald Reagan: A die-hard fan of baseball and a former radio broadcaster, Reagan attended a World Series game between the Baltimore Orioles and Philadelphia Phillies on October 11, 1983, but declined an opportunity to throw out the first pitch due to security reasons. Five years later, Reagan threw out two first pitches at Wrigley Field and then joined the legendary Harry Caray in the broadcast booth to announce the game for an inning and a half. "You know, in a few months, I'm going to be out of work," joked the outgoing president, who had once re-created games on radio, "and I thought I might as well audition."

Where did hot rods originate?

A Victorious American GIs returned from World War II ready to kick up their heels. They had fought hard, and once they got back, they wanted to play hard. They had money to burn, having saved their military pay for the day when the war would be over. For many, the mechanical skills they had honed during the conflict prepared them for the perfect pastime—hot-rodding.

Excess cash, combined with the first automobiles to be manufactured in the country in five years, created a boom in new car sales across the United States. But instead of merely junking their old sedans, people began to tinker under the hood and chop the bodies of these beaters.

The term hot rod most likely derived from hot roadster, and that's exactly what these cars were. These supercharged flying flivvers cropped up from coast to coast. But the center of this new diversion was Southern California, where warm weather and open land combined to make the perfect spot for racing.

The area north of Los Angeles, near the towns of Glendale, Pasadena, and Burbank, was covered with dry lake beds. The miles of barren land became the meeting place for gearheads and their thundering machines. Abandoned military airport runways were also natural racetrack straightaways, giving hot rods the chance to flex their metallic muscles in exciting drag races.

The phenomenon was not lost on people such as Wally Parks, who founded the National Hot Rod Association (NHRA) in 1951; the organization focused on safety and innovation. Magazines such as *Hot Rod* (which premiered in 1948) also supported action that was based on quality and care.

Unable to contain the growing craze, southern California gave up its hold on hot-rodding as it spread across the country. But areas such as the Midwest and New England were short on dry lake beds, so hot rods took to the streets of America, forcing police officers to chase down these speedsters.

 When was AstroTurf invented?

A Dubbed the eighth wonder of the world, the Houston Astrodome was renowned not only for its innovative design and remarkable roof but also for the artificial grass that covered its playing surface and forever changed the face of sports.

The synthetic substance that eventually became known as AstroTurf was originally designed as an urban playing surface meant to replace the concrete and brick that covered the recreation areas in city schoolyards. It was developed by employees of the Chemstrand Company, a subsidiary of Monsanto Industries, leading innovators in the development of synthetic fibers for use in carpeting.

In 1962, Dr. Harold Gores, the first president of Ford Foundation's Educational Facilities Laboratories, commissioned Monsanto to create an artificial playing surface that was wear-resistant, cost-efficient, comfortably cushioned, and traction tested. Two years later, the company introduced a synthetic surface called ChemGrass and installed it at the Moses Brown School, a private educational facility in Providence, Rhode Island. The new product met each of Dr. Gores's criteria except one: It was expensive to produce and wasn't a viable substitute for cement on playgrounds. However, it soon found a new home and a new name.

In 1965, the Astrodome, the world's first domed stadium, opened in Houston, Texas, featuring a glass-covered roof that allowed real grass to grow inside the dome. However, the athletes that used the facility complained they couldn't follow the path of the ball because of the glare caused by the glass. Painting the glass killed both the glare and the grass, so the lifeless lawn was replaced in 1966 with the revolutionary ChemGrass, which was quickly dubbed AstroTurf.

The new turf was a resounding success, and it soon became the desired surface for both indoor and outdoor stadiums. Dozens of high schools in the United States now have artificial playing surfaces.

When and where was NASCAR founded?

A The 1930s and 1940s saw a new breed of driver tearing up the back roads of the American South. Young, highly skilled, and full of brass, these road rebels spent their nights outwitting and outrunning federal agents as they hauled 60-gallon payloads of illegal moonshine liquor from the mountains to their eager customers in the cities below. In this dangerous game, speed and control made all the difference. The bootleggers spent as much time tinkering under their hoods as they did prowling the roads. A typical bootleg car might be a Ford Coupe with a 454 Cadillac engine, heavy-duty suspension, and any number of other modifications meant to keep the driver and his illicit cargo ahead of John Law.

With all that tes-
tosterone and
horsepower
bundled to-
gether, it was
inevitable that
these wild hares

would compete to see who had the fastest car and the steeliest
nerve. A dozen or more of them would get together on weekends
in an open field and spend the afternoon testing each other's skills,
often passing a hat among the spectators who came to watch. Promoters saw the potential in these events, and before long organized
races were being held all across the South. As often as not, though,
the promoters lit out with the receipts halfway through the race, and
the drivers saw nothing for their efforts.

Seeking to bring both legitimacy and profitability to the sport, driver
and race promoter William "Bill" Henry Getty France Sr. organized
a meeting of his colleagues at the Ebony Bar in Daytona Beach,
Florida, on December 14, 1947. Four days of haggling and back-
slapping led to the formation of the National Association for Stock
Car Auto Racing (NASCAR), with France named as its first president. The group held its inaugural race in 1948, on the well-known
half-sand, half-asphalt track at Daytona. Over the next two decades, the upstart organization built a name for itself on the strength
of its daring and charismatic drivers. Junior Johnson, Red Byron,
Curtis Turner, Lee Petty, and the Flock Brothers—Bob, Fonty, and
Tim—held regular jobs (some still running moonshine) and raced the
circuit in their spare time. And these legendary pioneers were some
colorful characters: For example, Tim Flock occasionally raced with
a pet monkey named Jocko Flocko, who sported a crash helmet and
was strapped into the passenger seat.

During these early years, NASCAR was viewed as a distinctly Southern enterprise. In the early 1970s, however, Bill France Jr. took control of the organization from his father, and things began to change. The younger France negotiated network television deals that brought the racetrack into the living rooms of Middle America. In 1979, CBS presented the first flag-to-flag coverage of a NASCAR event, and it was a doozy. Race leaders Cale Yarborough and Donnie Allison entered a bumping duel on the last lap that ended with both cars crashing on the third turn. As Richard Petty moved up from third to take the checkered flag, a fight broke out between Yarborough and Allison's brother Bobby. America was hooked.

France also expanded the sport's sponsorship beyond automakers and parts manufacturers. Tobacco giant R. J. Reynolds bought its way in, as did countless other purveyors of everyday household items, including Tide, Lowe's Hardware, Kellogg's Cereal, the Cartoon Network, Nextel, and Coca-Cola. Today, NASCAR vehicles and their beloved drivers are virtually moving billboards. Plastered with the logos of their sponsors as they speed around the track, Jeff Gordon, Dale Earnhardt Jr., Tony Stewart, Bobby Labonte, and their fellow daredevils draw the eyes of some 75 million regular fans and support a multibillion-dollar industry that outearns professional baseball, basketball, and hockey combined.

Q When was miniature golf invented?

A Miniature golf has been described as a novelty game, but it requires the same steady hands, analytical observation, and maneuvering as regular golf.

In their infancy, miniature golf courses were designed the same as full-size courses but were built at one-tenth the size, much like the popular par-3 courses of today. In 1916, James Barber of Pinehurst, North Carolina, created a miniature golf course that resembles the game played today. He dubbed his design "Thistle Dhu," supposedly a twist on the phrase "This'll do." Barber's course was an intricate maze of geometric shapes coupled with symmetric walkways, fountains, and planters.

Until 1922, mini-golf courses used live grass—just like the real game—and were subject to the same grooming needs and growing woes. That all changed when a man named Thomas McCulloch Fairbairn prepared a mixture of cottonseed hull—or mulch, sand, oil, and green dye—and used the concoction to resurface the miniature golf course he was designing. The first artificial putting green was born.

The game boomed for the next few years, with hundreds of miniature golf outlets opening around the country, including 150 rooftop courses in New York City alone. The arrival of the Great Depression severed the popularity of the pastime, and its growth remained stagnant until 1938 when brothers Joseph and Robert R. Taylor Sr. revitalized the game. The Taylors redesigned the sport by adding complicated obstacles such as windmills, castles, and wishing wells to increase the competitive enjoyment. Today, international miniature golf tournaments are held around the world. It's safe to say that the inventor of miniature golf hit a hole in one!

 Who was the first famous mascot?

 Part cheerleader, part contortionist, and part comedian, the mascot was inspired by the "fowl" play of a college student.

The colorful and enthusiastic mascots that provide comic relief and intermission entertainment at sporting events have become as essential to the games as snacks and sodas. Most of these individuals are talented athletes in their own rights, as dexterity in gymnastics, dance, and occasional stunts are vital ingredients of their performances.

The first mascot to gain notoriety for his amusing antics was a farcical fowl known as the San Diego Chicken. In 1974, a San Diego State University student named Ted Giannoulas was hired by a local radio station to dress like a chicken and hand out Easter eggs at the San Diego Zoo. Giannoulas's shtick was so popular among the children that he decided to attend San Diego Padres' baseball games and act as the team's "unofficial" mascot. The Chicken attracted worldwide acclaim—in fact, the mascot was named one of the 100 most powerful people in sports for the 20th century by *Sporting News Magazine*. Soon, most professional sports teams were using mascots to entertain, amuse, and fire up the fans.

The first official sideline mascot wasn't a gaily garbed goliath or dapperly draped demon, but it was definitely a beast. In 1889, Yale University enlisted an English bulldog named Handsome Dan to slobber along the sidelines and support the college football team, which became known as the Bulldogs.

Q When were zambonis invented?

 Before Frank Joseph Zamboni Jr. invented his self-propelled ice resurfacing machine, cleaning and clearing a sheet of ice was laborious, time-consuming, and inefficient.

Zamboni, an amateur inventor and the owner/operator of the Iceland Skating Rink in Paramount, California, needed a new method for sweeping the ice surface of his rink. Artificial ice rinks were still a novelty when Zamboni opened his facility in 1939, and it took a team of three people to repair and resurface the ice after it was gouged by hundreds of gliders, a procedure that could take up to ninety minutes.

Zamboni came up with an idea for a motorized machine that could do all the necessary work—sweep, scrape, and saturate—and could be operated by one man. He stripped an old Jeep down to its nuts, bolts, and bare underbody chassis and placed a blade on the under train to shave the ice smooth. He devised a device to sweep up the shavings and deposit the icy debris into a tank that melted the scrapings and used the water to rinse the rink. After several attempts and numerous prototypes, he perfected the "mechanical monster" and it became a tourist attraction in its own right.

 In 1950, Sonja Henie, a three-time Olympic figure skating champion and one of Hollywood's top box-office attractions, was rehearsing her new Hollywood Ice Revue at the Iceland when she saw the revolutionary resurfacer at work. She commissioned Zamboni to build her a new model for her upcoming performances in Chicago. That endorsement allowed Zamboni to mass-produce the machines that now bear his name.

Zamboni does a slick business. In 2014, the company web site noted that they have produced over 10,000 Zamboni machines. And they're definitely part of popular culture—Frank Zamboni was remembered in 2013 by an interactive Google Doodle where Googlers could drive a playable machine around a rink!

Q Where did the trampoline come from?

A If postcards sold in the Anchorage, Alaska, airport are to be believed, the genesis of the trampoline can be traced all the way to the Arctic Circle. The tourist tokens show Alaska Natives stretching a piece of walrus skin and using the taut tarp to toss each other in the air. It's a good story, but it's not true.

It was actually an athlete and coach from the University of Iowa who created the first manufactured version of the rebounding rig known as the trampoline. During the winter of 1934, George Nissen, a tumbler on the college gymnastics team, and Larry Griswold, his assistant coach, were discussing ways to add some flair to their rather staid sport. The two men were intrigued by the possibilities presented by the buoyant nature of the safety nets used by trapeze artists.

Griswold and Nissen constructed an iron frame and covered it with a large canvas, using springs to connect the cloth to the frame. The apparatus was an effective training device and a popular attraction among the kids who flocked to the local YMCA to watch Nissen perform his routines. The pair of co-creators eventually formed the Griswold-Nissen Trampoline & Tumbling Company and started producing the first commercially available and affordable trampolines.

Nissen can also claim fame for attaching a name to his pliant production. While on a tour of Mexico in the late 1930s, Nissen discovered the Spanish word for springboard was *el trampolin*. Intrigued by the sound of the word, he Anglicized the spelling, and the trampoline was born. Nissen promoted his invention heavily; he even rented a kangaroo for a demonstration in New York's Central Park.

In 2000, trampolining graduated from acrobatic activity to athletic achievement when it was officially recognized as a medal-worthy Olympic sport in Sydney, Australia. Nissen, then in his mid-80's, sat in the audience.

Q How did the Ironman Triathlon start?

A "Faster, higher, stronger" may be the motto for the modern Olympic Games, but it's also an apt description for the athletes who stretched the boundaries of human endurance and initiated the Ironman competition.

The old cliché "anything you can do, I can do better," along with a spirited discussion over the true meaning of "better," ultimately led to the creation of the Ironman Triathlon. During the awards ceremony for the 1977 Oahu Perimeter Relay, a running race for five-person teams held in Hawaii, the winning participants, among them both runners and swimmers, became engrossed in a debate over which athletes were more fit.

As both sides tossed biting barbs, rousing rhetoric, and snide snippets back and forth, a third party entered the fray. Navy Commander John Collins, who was listening to the spirited spat, mentioned that a recent article in *Sports Illustrated* magazine claimed that bike racers, especially Tour de France winner Eddy Merckx, had the highest recorded "oxygen uptake" of any athlete ever measured, insinuating that cyclists were more fit than anyone. Collins and his wife, Judy, suggested the only way to truly bring the argument to a rightful conclusion was to arrange an extreme endurance competition, combining a swim of considerable length, a bike race of taxing duration, and a marathon foot race.

The first Ironman Triathlon was held on February 18, 1978, in Honolulu, Hawaii. Participants were invited to "Swim 2.4 miles! Bike 112 miles! Run 26.2 miles! Brag for the rest of your life." This rousing slogan has since become the registered trademark of the event.

But the Ironman competition was not the first triathlon event. The first competition to combine swimming (500-yard race), bike racing (5-mile course), and running (2.8 miles) was held on September 25, 1974, in San Diego, California.

Q How did modern bowling develop?

 Over the millennia there have been many games similar to bowling. The ancient Egyptians played something very much like it; Moses' pharaoh may well have had a gilded bowling shirt. In colonial times, the little men played ninepin while lulling

Rip Van Winkle into a two-decade sleep. That game was played on an alley consisting of a single plank. The modern game grew directly from that humble pursuit, thanks to the ingenuity of German immigrants who popularized the sport in America.

"It was part of their religious culture. They used to have it at church festivals centuries ago," says Milwaukee bowling historian Doug Schmidt, author of *They Came to Bowl.*

As Germans started landing in New York in the 1800s, they quickly set up bowling clubs. Eventually, these immigrants started making their way to the Midwest, and bowling followed them. Tavern owners, among others, began installing bowling lanes.

Originally, it was a game of ninepin set up in a diamond formation. Gambling was a popular feature, and as a result the game was outlawed. The immigrants added another pin, changed the formation to a triangle, and satisfied the courts that it was a different game. Modern bowling was born—almost.

As strange as it may sound today, bowling was originally outdoor fun, played in the sun. In the 1850s, "the only bowlers were Germans and the only alleys were crude ones at the picnic groves and other German resorts," wrote historian Andrew Rohm in 1904. In Milwaukee, Wisconsin, in the late 1800s, brewers Frederick Pabst and Frederick Miller each opened their own private pleasure parks and pavilions. There, the German biergarten tradition incorporated their favorite game. Gradually, for year-round enjoyment, bowling moved inside.

(Nor is that Wisconsin's only claim to bowling fame. Milwaukee could be called the capital of bowling—it's home to the United

States Bowling Congress. And in 1930, Wisconsinite Jennie Hover-son became the first woman to bowl a perfect game in the history of league bowling, though she was not recognized for it until later.)

For much of its American history, bowling was a northern pastime. Besides sexism, nationally there was bowling bigotry along racial lines. African Americans were not allowed into sanctioned league bowling until 1951, four years after Jackie Robinson broke the color barrier in baseball, although African Americans were enjoying the game by the 1940s. They had come to the north in search of factory jobs and found themselves near taverns with bowling alleys. Many became well-known bowlers.

Today, bowling's best features remain as satisfying as ever: The cost is low, the rules are simple, and the bowling alley provides all of the equipment. Then there's the satisfying, almost-musical crash of the maplewood pins. And what other sport has ten second chances? There's also the camaraderie, or, in other words, waiting.

"The big advantage is that it's a team sport that promotes social interaction," says Schmidt. With other games, such as football or baseball, "you're either out on the field or on the sidelines, where in bowling you're sitting around connecting with each other while you're waiting for your turn."

Q Where did softball originate?

 Like many American communities, Chicago has numerous public parks dotted with ball fields where weekend warriors gather for league softball games in the summer. But Chicagoans play their own unique version of the game.

Though softball is a popular recreational sport all over the nation, it was born is Chicago. The first softball was made there in 1887 by George Hancock, who fashioned it from (naturally enough) an old boxing glove and used it to create an indoor version of baseball. By the early 1900s, the sport was being played outdoors and had begun to spread across the Midwest. Several variations of the game developed, with the key difference being the size of the ball. The first national championships—held in Chicago in 1933 during the Century of Progress Exposition and won by a Chicago team—used a 14-inch ball.

The American Softball Association was formed that same year, and the sport took off nationwide. Most other areas quickly moved to a version often called kitten ball, which uses a 12-inch ball and allows the fielders to wear mitts. Wimps! This remains the most well known version today, having been popularized through college teams. Chicagoans, however, stayed fiercely loyal to the original game and embraced the 16-inch mush ball and bare-handed fielding. After all, with a glove, where's the challenge?

The sport's heyday during the 1930s and 1940s centered around the professional Windy City League, which regularly garnered coverage in the local sports sections and sometimes drew higher attendance than the city's two major-league baseball teams. Though the Windy City League folded decades ago, their game remains the most popular bat-and-ball sport in the city today. According to DeBeer and

Sons, the company that manufactures the 16-inch ball under the name Clincher, 85 percent of their product is sold in the Chicago area.

Year after year, the city is able to support dozens of leagues with hundreds of teams that draw thousands of players from all walks of life. Teams are usually coed, and many players remain active in the game until their 50s—two advantages of the larger ball, which travels slowly no matter how hard you hit it, allowing a wider array of people to participate. The large ball also means that offensively it's a game of precision rather than power. Home runs do happen but not that often; runs are scored primarily by advancing the runners through well-placed singles and doubles. The rules make that harder by calling for a ten-player lineup for each team rather than the traditional nine. The extra fielder—called the short center—is stationed in between second base and center field to catch the all-too-common short fly ball.

The absence of mitts requires a higher level of skill among the fielders, who must be adept at handling the unwieldy ball. On the downside, mush ball aficionados perpetually suffer from jammed and broken fingers that are proudly earned and stoically shrugged off while playing defense.

For many of the thousands of Chicagoans who take to the fields every summer, the game is a way to get some exercise, enjoy the outdoors, and relax with friends. But a great many players are lifelong devotees of the sport. Some belong to several teams and play three or four games a week—sometimes even two in a night on opposite ends of the city, which is no small feat in this sprawling metropolis. And there is no doubt the city as a whole takes its homegrown game seriously. The public school system has accepted it as a lettered sport in high schools, and there is even a Chicago Softball Hall of Fame that honors local legends of the game, such as Lewa "Rocco" Yacilla, the beloved Windy City League pitcher who earned more than 3,000 career wins and threw the only no-hitter in the league's history.

Q **Who wrote "Take Me Out to the Ball Game"?**

A Next to the national anthem, the song most associated with the game of baseball is "Take Me Out to the Ball Game," an early-20th-century song usually played during the seventh-inning stretch. Ironically, it was written by two men who had never attended a baseball game, and wouldn't until years after they wrote the song.

Jack Norworth wrote the words in 1908, after seeing a sign that said, "Baseball Today—Polo Grounds." While most people now only know and sing the chorus, the song does have verses as well—they tell the story of Katie Casey (called Nelly Kelly in later versions), a baseball-loving girl who knows exactly where she wants her beau to take her on a date. A knowledgeable girl, Katie cheered on the players and also "told the umpire he was wrong / All along / Good and strong."

Musicians Albert Von Tilzer added the music to Jack Norworth's lyrics, and the song gained popularity in vaudeville acts. It actually wasn't played at a baseball game until years later, although now it's played at nearly every baseball game in the country.

Incidentally, the snack mentioned in the song, Cracker Jack, dates back to the mid-1890s.

How did football become the game it is today?

A The game of football today bears little resemblance to the disorganized brawls of the late 1800s. Here are just some of the milestones that shaped the game we know today.

1861: The first documented football game (essentially rugby) is played at the University of Toronto.

1869: An era begins as Princeton travels to Rutgers for a rousing game of "soccer football." The field is 120 yards long by 75 yards wide, about 25 percent longer and wider than the modern field. It plays more like soccer than modern football, and with 25 players on a side, the field is a crowded place. Rutgers prevails 6–4.

1874: McGill University (of Montreal) and Harvard play a hybrid version of rugby. The rule changes soon affect the game as it's played in the United States.

1875: The game ball officially becomes an egg-shape rugby ball.

Henceforth the field is supposed to be 100 yards long by 53.5 yards wide (though this won't be fully standard for some years), so teams are cut to 15 players per side. Referees are added to the game.

1876: With the addition of the crossbar, goal posts now look like an H.

1880–1885: The modern game's fundamentals are introduced. A downs system goes into use (five yards in three downs equals a first down), along with the scrimmage line and yard lines. Teams are now eleven on a side. Major changes to scoring: A field goal is worth five points, a touchdown and conversion count four points each, and a safety is two points. The first play-calling signals and planned plays come about.

1892: Desperate to beat the Pittsburgh Athletic Club team, Allegheny Athletic Association leaders create the professional football player by hiring Pudge Heffelfinger to play for their team. Heffelfinger plays a pivotal role in AAA's 4–0 victory.

1894: The officiating crew is increased to three: a referee and two bodyguards, also known as the umpire and linesman.

1896: Only one backfield man may now be in motion before the snap, and he can't be moving forward.

1897: A touchdown now counts as five points.

1902: College football is getting a little unbalanced as Michigan, having outscored its regular schedule 501–0, drubs Stanford 49–0 in the first Rose Bowl. The first African American professional football player takes the field: Charles Follis of the Shelby (Ohio) Athletic Club.

1905: Disgusted at the mortality rate among college football players, Teddy Roosevelt tells the Ivy League schools: "Fix this blood sport, or I'll ban it." Rules Committee (forerunner of the NCAA) comes into being and legalizes the forward pass, bans mass plays responsible for brutish pileups and deaths, establishes the neutral zone along the

line of scrimmage, and prohibits
players from locking arms.

1909: Now a field goal is worth
three points. This rule will stand,
but the distances, hash marks,
and goal posts will change many
more times. In Canada, the first
Grey Cup game is played—at this
phase, it's a collegiate event.

1910: Seven players must now be on the line of scrimmage when
the ball is snapped, establishing the basic offensive formation concept. The forward pass becomes commonplace in college football.

1912: Rules Committee determines that a touchdown is worth six
points, and it adds a fourth down. It is now practical to punt.

1921: Fans hear the first commercially sponsored radio broadcast of a game, with University of Pittsburgh beating West Virginia
21–13.

1922: The American Professional Football Association becomes the
National Football League (NFL).

1932: The NFL begins keeping statistics. Collegiate football doesn't
see the benefits of official stat keeping until 1937.

1933: There is a major NFL rule change: The passer can throw
from anywhere behind scrimmage. (Before this, he had to be five
yards behind scrimmage.)

1934: The modern football takes its current shape after a couple of decades of gradual evolution from the egglike rugby ball.

1937: College football players must now have numbers on the fronts and backs of their jerseys.

1939: The Brooklyn Dodgers–Philadelphia Eagles game is the first to be beamed into the few New York homes that can afford TV sets in this late-Depression year. Helmets become mandatory in college football, and the pros follow within a decade.

1941: It's the end of the drop-kick score. Ray McLean boots a conversion off the turf in the NFL championship game. (Actually, it wasn't the last one kicked. In 2005, Doug Flutie created a sensation by doing it again.)

1946: The NFL's first major rival league, the All-America Football Conference (AAFC), begins play. It lasts four seasons, with the Cleveland Browns winning all four titles.

1950: Rules now permit unlimited free substitution, opening a hole for platoon football (exclusive offensive or defensive squads).

1951: First coast-to-coast TV broadcast of an NFL game as the Los Angeles Rams face the Cleveland Browns in the league championship game. Face masks show up in the college game.

1956: The NFL penalizes face masking (except for the ball carrier, who can be slammed to the turf by the face cage until 1960).

1958: In college football, a run or pass for conversion now counts two points.

1960: The American Football League (AFL), the NFL's new rival, begins play. Everyone derides it as inferior, just like the old AAFC.

1967: The NFL offsets goal posts with a recessed curved pole in a "slingshot" shape. Super Bowl I is played: The Green Bay Packers beat the Kansas City Chiefs, 35–10.

1970: The AFL wins the Super Bowl, then merges into the NFL, creating the biggest sports-marketing titan of all time. (Ten modern NFL teams trace heritage to the AFL.)

1974: The NFL adds sudden-death overtime for regular-season games, moves the goal posts to the back of the end zone, moves kickoffs back from the 40- to the 35-yard line, and spots the ball at the line of scrimmage for missed field goals beyond the 20. Pass defense rules now restrict defenders, opening up the air game.

1975: Kicker/quarterback George Blanda of the Oakland Raiders finally hangs up his cleats at the age of 48.

1979–1980: No more blocking below the waist on kicks, refs are to whistle a play dead when a player has the quarterback in a death grip but has not yet slammed him to the turf, and personal-foul rules tighten up.

1987: Arena Football League season starts with four teams: the Chicago Bruisers, Denver Dynamite, Pittsburgh Gladiators, and Washington Commandos.

1988: The NFL increases the play clock to 45 seconds between plays. Eventually this is shortened to 40 seconds. College still uses the 25-second play clock.

1991: The World League of American Football (WLAF)—history's first non–North American league—begins in Europe as a sort of NFL minor league. Europeans prefer soccer.

1994: Professional football institutes the option of either running or passing for two points (instead of kicking for one) after a touchdown.

1999: The NFL begins using an instant replay challenge system, eliminating officiating errors forever.

2007: The NFL Europa, successor to the WLAF, finally shuts down, as Europeans still prefer soccer.

Chapter 7
LANGUAGE AND LINGO

Q **When did fans from Wisconsin first call themselves Cheeseheads?**

A Of course, the term "Cheesehead" is used to describe the big, soft, triangular headwear seen at sporting events. However, "Cheesehead" also refers to the big, soft, diehard fans that wear them. It's hard to believe that the wildly popular hats originated as an insult from the fine citizens of Illinois. Exhilarated by their 1986 Super Bowl victory, Chicago Bears fans began making fun of their northern neighbors by referring to residents of the Dairy State as "Cheeseheads." But Wisconsinites didn't seem to take it personally, and they didn't take it lying down.

The rivalry escalated during baseball season, when Chicago White Sox fans mocked Brewers fans, chanting "Cheeseheads." Ralph Bruno of Milwaukee decided to take action. A cheese-lover himself, Bruno wanted to show the Illinois bullies, and his Wisconsin brethren, that there's really nothing wrong with being a Cheesehead.

In 1987, Bruno wore the first wedge-shape cheesehead to a Milwaukee Brewers game. It was fashioned from his mother's sofa cushion. The score of the game is irrelevant to the history that was made that day—the hat was a hit. Bruno got such a positive reaction from other fans that he started developing the idea immediately. In fact, by the next day, he was carving the master mold out of Styrofoam.

Combining elements of several cheese varieties, the Cheesehead is distinctive in its appearance. It has holes for Swiss cheese, the triangular shape associated with Gouda, and, of course, the yellow of Wisconsin cheddar. Bruno himself produced the original hats in his spare time. A pattern-maker for mechanical and industrial machinery, Bruno created his own equipment and begged help from family and friends.

Today, the headgear is so closely associated with football that it may surprise some to learn that the hats were originally produced primarily for baseball fans at County Stadium. That actually led to the first hybrid Cheesehead hat—shaped like a baseball cap. This came about after Brewers owner Bud Selig complained that the larger triangle-shape version obstructed the view for other fans.

At first, it was hard to get financial support for the business. The idea was intriguing to bankers but hardly a sure thing. In fact, most thought the headwear would only be a short-lived fad. Using credit cards, Bruno got the business up and running—just in time for the Packers' Super Bowl years.

Suddenly, the Cheesehead was the most sought-after hat in town. Well, in the state, actually. And the nationally televised Packers games helped increase demand for the hats throughout the Dairy State—and the image spread throughout the country.

Today, making Cheeseheads is a full-time job for Bruno, who manufactures a multitude of cheese products from his own company,

Foamation (found online at www.cheesehead.com, of course). The original hat was on display for a time at the Wisconsin Historical Society, and new ones are still rolling off the assembly line for a new generation of fans. Foamation has sold products in all 50 states and in more than 30 countries. Cheeseheads have been worn by high-profile politicians (what better way to win a vote in Wisconsin?) and celebrities.

You can still get the original Cheesehead wedge-shape hat, but now it comes in a youth version and an even smaller size for babies or pets. There are even mini Cheeseheads (measuring two inches from point to point) that are just perfect for your Barbie or GI Joe. There's also a patriotic Cheesehead in fashionable red, white, and blue—complete with stars and stripes.

Q What sport uses the terms "hammer" and "hogline"?

A It's an Olympic sport that takes place on ice—but it's not hockey. It involves broom, rocks, and some nifty terminology. Here's some information on curling, a sport that's akin to shuffleboard or bowling on ice.

Curling began in Scotland in the 1500s, played with river-worn stones. In the next century, enterprising curlers began to fit the stones with handles. With Canada's heavy Scottish influence and northerly climate, curling was a perfect fit. The Royal Montreal Curling Club began in 1807, and in 1927, Canada held its first national curling championship. Today, curling has millions of enthusiasts around the world. Canadian curlers routinely beat international competition, a source of brimming national pride.

The standard curling rink measures 146 feet by 15 feet. At each end are 12-foot-wide concentric rings called houses, the center of which is the button. There are four curlers on a team. Each throws two rocks (shoves them, rather; you don't really want to go airborne with a 44-pound granite rock) in an effort to get as close to the button as possible. When all eight players have thrown two rocks each, it concludes the end (analogous to a baseball inning). A game consists of eight or ten ends.

The goal is to knock the other team's rocks out of the house, and thus out of scoring position, while getting yours to hang around close to the button. After all throws, the team with the rock nearest the button scores a point for each of its rocks that's nearer the button than the opponent's nearest rock (and inside the house).

The players with the brooms, by the way, aren't trying to keep the ice clear of crud. The team skip (captain) determines strategy and advises the players using the brooms in the fine art of sweeping. Skips can guide the stone with surprising precision by skillfully sweeping in front of it with their brooms, but they can't touch (burn) that rock or any others in the process.

Curling is a game that values good sportsmanship. Curlers even call themselves for burns. When a team is so far behind it cannot win, it is considered proper sportsmanship to concede by removing gloves and shaking hands.

And here's some curling jargon, for the next time you drag out your broom and go to your local ice risk:

Bonspiel: a curling tournament

Draw: shot thrown to score

Hack: foot brace curlers push off from, like track sprinters

Hammer: last rock of the end (advantageous)

Hog line: blue line in roughly the same place as a hockey blue line. One must let go of the rock before crossing the near hog line—and the rock must cross the far hog line—or it's hogged (removed from play).

Pebble: water drops sprayed on the ice between ends, making the game more interesting

Takeout: shot meant to knock a rock out of play

Up! Whoa! Off! Hurry! Hard!: examples of orders the skip might call to the sweepers

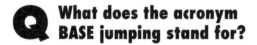 **What does the acronym BASE jumping stand for?**

A BASE jumping—an acronym for Building, Antenna, Span, Earth—is the practice of skydiving from these four different, ground-anchored points. "Span" in this context refers to bridges; "Earth" to gorges and cliffs (so no, just hopping off a rock won't count). The name comes from a group of jumpers led by Carl Boenis. His group's jump from El Capitan in Yosemite National Park set off the modern BASE jumping movement. Popularized by endorphin-junkies in the 1970s, the sport continues to grow despite inherent risks—and the fact that gaining permission to jump from certain places can be tricky. In the United States, for example, BASE jumping is not currently permitted in U.S. National Parks, although some people jump surreptitiously.

Though no single venue is typical, West Virginia's famed New River Gorge Bridge is revered as a glorious step-off spot. In fact, New River Gorge is the site of an annual celebration, Bridge Day. Once there, jumpers toss themselves into the 876-foot high abyss. Freefall time before chutes open? About four seconds. Time from takeoff to "splat!" if they don't? Approximately eight seconds.

Since 1981, more than 200 unlucky BASE. jumpers have been killed pursuing the sport. Unfortunately, that list includes Carl Boenish, who died in 1986, only two days after setting a record for height on a jump.

Q What sport's name means "the bishop's staff"?

A Algonquins called the sport *baggataway* and the Iroquois called it *teewaarathon*. We can thank French Canadians for the name by which we know the sport today: "La crosse" means "the bishop's staff," because that's what the stick looked like.

Lacrosse is Canada's national summer sport and is the fastest growing high school and college sport in the United States. Along with basketball, it is arguably the most North American game there is—First Peoples/Native Americans invented it. Natives played the game to honor the Great Spirit or revered elders, or to celebrate. Lacrosse also served a diplomatic role. Suppose you were a Mohawk elder and you learned that the Oneidas were fishing on your side of the lake (violating your long-standing agreement).

Rather than sending your warriors to fight the Oneida, you'd send an emissary to challenge them to settle the dispute with a *teewaarathon* match. These early games, which were quite violent, took place on fields that were miles long and involved as many as 1,000 participants.

Europeans' first record of a lacrosse match dates to the 1630s in southern Ontario, when missionary Jean de Brébeuf watched the Hurons play. By the 1800s, the game was popular with French Canadian settlers. In 1867, the same year Canada became a dominion, Canadian dentist W. George Beers standardized the rules of lacrosse. By 1900, the Canadian game had spread well across its native land and into the United States, with men's and women's versions.

There are two primary forms of lacrosse today: box (indoor) and field (outdoor). Box lacrosse is largely a Canadian sport, but Canadians also compete well in men's and women's field lacrosse. The game values speed and agility above brawn. The crosse (stick) takes skill to manipulate as players move the ball around.

In men's lacrosse, these are the standard positions:

Attack: There are three attackers on the field at one time. The attackers use "short-sticks" and must demonstrate good stick-handling with both hands; they must know where their teammates are at all times and be able to handle the pressure of opposing defense. Attackers score most of the goals.

Defense: Three defensive players with "long-poles" and one long-stick midfielder are allowed on the field at a time, using their sticks to throw checks and trying to dislodge the ball. One of the "long-poles" may also play midfield as a strategic defender, also known as a long-stick middie. Teams usually use this to anticipate losing the face-off and to be stronger on defense.

Midfield: Three "middies" are allowed on the field at once. There are two types of midfielders, defensive and offensive. The two can rotate by running off the sidelines. Midfielders are allowed to use short-sticks and up to one long-pole. While on offense, three short-sticks are generally used for their superior stick-handling. While on defense, two short-sticks are used with one long-pole. Some teams have a designated face-off middie who takes the majority of face-offs and is usually quickly substituted after the face-off is complete.

Goalkeeper: Goalies try to prevent the ball from getting into the goal, and they also direct the team defense. A goalkeeper needs to be tough both physically and mentally, and he has to be loud enough to call the position of the ball at all times so the defense can concentrate on where the players are.

Play flow is similar to hockey or soccer; a team tries to control the ball and send it past a goaltender into the net. Fouls are similar to those in hockey, as is the penalty box. So if you're in the mood for a physical, speedy, demanding game that requires the toughness of rugby and the stamina of soccer, pick up your "bishop's staff" and start training!

Q In hockey, why is scoring three goals called a hat trick?

A The sports world is full of weird, wonderful jargon. Third base in baseball is called "the hot corner." In football, a deep pass thrown up for grabs is known as a "Hail Mary." In hockey, scoring three goals is labeled a "hat trick." The first term makes sense, the second one kind of makes sense, and the third one is completely baffling. Throughout most of hockey's history, players didn't wear helmets, let alone hats. What gives?

Etymologists agree that the term "hat trick" originated in cricket, a British game that few Americans care about or understand. Evidently, back in the mid-1850s, when a cricket "bowler" captured three consecutive "wickets," he earned a free hat. Though we have no idea what that means, it still raises the question: How did the term "hat trick" infiltrate the lexicon of hockey?

As legend has it, hockey's use of "hat trick" originated in the early 1940s with a Toronto haberdasher (someone who sells hats) named Sammy Taft. The story goes that a Chicago Blackhawks forward named Alex Kaleta visited Taft's shop one day in search of a new fedora, only to find that Taft's hats were too pricey for his meager professional athlete's salary (my, how times have changed).

Taft, feeling generous, offered to give Kaleta the hat for free if he could score three goals in that evening's game against the Toronto

Maple Leafs. Kaleta did, and the hat was his. Taft, sensing a potential marketing boon, made a standing offer to any player who could
score three goals in a Maple Leafs home game. Sometimes he even
threw the prize hat onto the ice after the third goal. The hat-tossing
became a fad, and soon other fans—apparently far wealthier than
poor Kaleta—were tossing their hats onto the ice.

For many hockey fans, any excuse to throw something onto the ice
is cause for celebration. Besides hats, octopuses have been tossed
onto the rink by fans in Detroit, and in Florida the lovely tradition of
throwing rats onto the ice began after a Panthers player scored two
goals in a game after killing a rat in the locker room.

It's a far cry from the heart-warming tradition started (the story goes)
by Sammy Taft. Then again, the whole concept of hockey in Florida
is pretty weird in itself.

Q Why are ineligible college athletes called redshirts?

A Ask Star Trek fans what a "redshirt" is, and they'll tell you
that it's a term that's used to describe a stock character who
is introduced into a storyline, only to be killed by the end of the episode. Ask Italians what a "redshirt" is, and they'll point to a portrait
of Giuseppe Garibaldi as they hum a few bars of Italy's national
anthem. Ask college football fans what a "redshirt" is, and they'll
stare at you blankly for a few minutes before asking you to pass the
chips and dip.

This is not so much a reflection of the IQ of the average football
fan as it is of the general confusion surrounding the term "redshirt."
Part of the problem is this: Although the term is bandied about quite

often in discussions of college sports, "redshirt" isn't an official term of the governing body of college athletics, the National Collegiate Athletic Association (NCAA). Furthermore, try as you might, you won't find any college athletes sitting on the sidelines actually wearing red shirts—unless red is the color of their uniform, of course.

Much of the confusion is rooted in the NCAA's rules of eligibility for college athletes. Essentially, all college athletes are given, upon initial enrollment, five years to complete four years of competition. Because of this rule, some college athletes skip a season of play in order to extend their eligibility. In order to earn a fifth year of eligibility, the player must not participate in any sanctioned competition during the skipped season. Not one play in a football game, not one pitch in a baseball game—any participation whatsoever uses up one year of eligibility. There are hundreds of detailed rules that further define eligibility; in fact, many college athletic departments have entire divisions devoted to merely interpreting and applying the rules for their own players.

College athletes might choose to sit out a season for a number of reasons, including injury, academic issues, or because the player isn't physically and/or mentally ready to play at the college level. These athletes are allowed to practice with the team, essentially making the skipped season an extended training session.

When this practice first started in college sports, these athletes would wear red shirts during practice to differentiate them from eligible players, hence the term. The word entered the lexicon in

September 1950, according to the *Oxford English Dictionary*, when it was used in a Birmingham, Alabama, newspaper article.

Nowadays, red-shirting is a common practice. College sports are multibillion-dollar industry, and the players are auditioning for multi-million-dollar jobs in the professional ranks. So the next time you're watching the big game at a buddy's house and the announcer refers to a player as a redshirt freshman, you can enlighten your friends about the term and its origin. Just make sure to pass the chips first.

Q How did the Super Bowl get its name?

A Today, Super Bowl Sunday is practically a national holiday. Fans and nonfans alike gather for huge meals and expensive commercial breaks. The championship game, which began in 1967, helped boost the popularity of American football.

Throughout its history, the National Football League (NFL) faced rival competing leagues. Each time, the NFL would emerge the victor. But that all changed with the creation of the American Football League (AFL). The upstart AFL successfully wooed players from the NFL and helped lay the foundation for modern American football.

The AFL got its start when the NFL rebuffed Lamar Hunt, the son of an oilman, in his bid for an expansion team. In response, Hunt went on to found the AFL and the Dallas Texans in 1960. The league consisted of eight teams and was bankrolled by other would-be owners who had been unable to procure expansion franchises in the NFL.

While the NFL tacitly enforced unwritten quotas for African American players, the AFL actively recruited them. The younger league also competed for top college talent, nabbing Heisman-winner Billy Cannon in 1959 and Joe Namath in 1964. In 1966, new AFL commissioner Al Davis actively wooed players from the NFL. This practice promoted bidding wars for players between teams in the two leagues.

Hunt and Dallas Cowboys President Texas "Tex" Schramm Jr. met privately to discuss the possibility of merging the two leagues. On January 15, 1967, the champion team of each league met in the AFL–NFL Championship Game to determine an all-around winner. Suggesting some consistency with the college "bowl" games (e.g., the Rose Bowl, the Orange Bowl) used to crown regional champions, Hunt recommended "Super Bowl," a reference to the Super Ball toy his kids enjoyed.

The name stuck but was not officially used until Super Bowl III in 1969. (The 1967 and '68 championship games are only called Super Bowl I and II retroactively; at the time, they were called the AFL–NFL Championship Games.) The Super Bowl trophy was named the Vince Lombardi Trophy following the legendary coach's death in 1970.

 What was basketball almost called?

Some sports have murky origins, long lost in history. Basketball, though, has a clear provenance that can be traced back to one man. Born in 1861, James Naismith was raised in the small Canadian village of Bennie's Corners, Ontario. Naismith grew up both morally and physically fit, performing heavy chores, walking five miles across frozen fields to school, and playing with his friends near the village blacksmith shop.

Later, at McGill University in Montreal, Naismith earned degrees in philosophy and Hebrew while playing hard-hitting sports such as rugby and lacrosse. Despite the prevailing Victorian opinion that sports were violent and vice-ridden, James Naismith was convinced that sports could be used to instill good values. He attended International Young Men's Christian Association Training School in Springfield, Massachusetts, where he worked toward his divinity degree while teaching physical education.

In 1891, the school's superintendent challenged Naismith to develop an indoor sport that would keep the boys busy during the cold winter months and that would be "fair for all players, and free of rough play."

Naismith carefully planned this new sport. Games with larger balls were less violent, he noted, so he chose to use a soccer ball. Abuse between players occurred more frequently when the ball was near the goal. Naismith's new game would have goals placed above the player's heads. He also noticed that injuries occurred most often between players in motion. The players in his game would stop as soon as they had possession of the ball.

To solve the problem of how to get the ball into the goal, Naismith showed his students how to throw using a lobbing motion he and his friends developed while playing a game called "Duck on a Rock" in Bennie's Corners. Armed with their "Duck on a Rock" skills, Naismith's students played the first game of basketball in December 1891, using wooden peach baskets nailed to the walls of the gym.

School members called for the game to be named "Naismithball" after its inventor. He stuck to his guns, though, so the game became known as "Basket Ball."

Q What was the origin of the word umpire?

 This term derives from the 14th-century Middle English word *noumpere*. It evolved over the years to *oumpere* and finally to *nonper*, where the word breaks down into two parts: non for "not" and per for "equal." In short, the word meant "not an equal." It was used to describe the third man called in to settle disagreements. Interestingly, that is why there are an uneven number of umpires in sports—so someone always has the deciding vote.

While we're thinking of umpires, here's some trivia about early umpires...

The first National League baseball game officiated at by an umpire was played between Boston and Philadelphia in 1876. The umpire's name was William McLean; he'd previously umpired National Association games.

Three years later, in 1879, umpires were empowered to give fines for illegal acts.

1885 brought about a safety innovation, as umpires began to wear chest protectors.

The first umpire to throw someone out of a World Series game was Thomas Connolly, who tossed out Frank Chance, the manager of the Chicago Cubs, in 1910.

Q Why is the St. Louis baseball team called the Cardinals, even though Missouri's state bird is the bluebird?

A For more than eighty years, the image of two cardinals perched on a baseball bat has been the logo of the St. Louis Cardinals, one of the most successful and popular franchises in Major League Baseball. Cardinals greats from Stan Musial to Bob Gibson to Albert Pujols have worn the famous image across their chests. But why would the most famous sports franchise in the state—in which the eastern bluebird is the official bird—be associated with the cardinal?

The answer to this quirky question has nothing to do with birds at all. When St. Louis's ball club joined the National League in 1892, it was known as the Browns, and its players were decked out, predictably, in brown-trimmed duds. In 1899, however, new owners decided to change the franchise's nickname to the Perfectos and give the players new uniforms that were accented with red trim and red-striped socks.

At one game, according to St. Louis lore, sportswriter Willie McHale overheard a female fan say this of the team's uniforms: "What a lovely shade of cardinal." At the time, it was not unusual for reporters to refer to the teams they covered by unofficial nicknames of their own creation. McHale started referring to the clumsily named Perfectos as the Cardinals in his columns, and the new moniker proved so popular that the team officially changed its name for the 1900 season.

The association between the shade of red and the creature of the same color dates back to at least 1922, when the team adopted the first incarnation of the "birds on a bat" logo. These days, the identity of the team is intertwined with the bird, and it's impossible to see one without thinking of the other.

State birds weren't even established until 1927, when seven states (including Missouri) adopted legislation that named an official avian representative. The eastern bluebird, which is common east of the Rocky Mountains, symbolizes happiness and the coming of spring in Missouri. Unlike the cardinal, which is usually a year-round resident, the eastern bluebird normally appears in northern Missouri each February and heads south around November. On March 30, 1927, the Missouri legislature established that the "native 'bluebird' is selected for and shall be known as the official bird of the state of Missouri."

The cardinal is the state bird in seven other states, including Illinois, which is the home of St. Louis's biggest baseball rival, the Chicago Cubs.

How did the term "bogey" find its way into golf?

All sorts of golf terms have fuzzy histories. This is hardly surprising, since the game is more than five hundred years old and is generally accepted to have begun with a gang of Scots whacking the ball across sheep pastures.

Amazingly enough, we not only can pin down the time that the word "bogey" was brought into play in golf, but we can also cite the specific place. The odd wrinkle, though, is that the story behind the term seems to depend on which side of the pond you're on, and the origin of the word itself is unknown. By the way, when the term came into use, a "bogey" meant what golfers now call "par."

According to the British Golf Museum, "bogey" originated from "the mythical golfer, Colonel Bogey, a player of high amateur standard who was held to play every hole of a given course in the standard stroke score." The version of events given by the United States Golf Association (USGA) says that the term comes from "a song that was popular in the British Isles in the early 1890s."

Whether the ruling body of golf in America knows more about the gent known as Bogey than the folks who are thought to have invented golf is open to debate (perhaps they are both correct), but there is agreement on both sides of the Atlantic about when and where the term and the sport got together.

The use of the term "bogey" in golf began in Norfolk, England, around 1890. The Great Yarmouth Golf Club adopted a suggestion from Hugh Rotherham, secretary of the Coventry Golf Club, that there should be a standard to judge the number of shots a good golfer ought to score on any given hole that did not rely on the score of one's opponents. For centuries, golf scoring was based on match play—all that mattered was that a golfer's score per hole was lower than the opponent's. Later, in the mid-1700s, the total number of strokes were counted but were still compared to the scores of other players. Rotherham's fixed score, which he called a "ground score," was accepted and then put into use.

Golfing authority Robert Browning, editor of *Golfing* magazine for forty-five years, reports that as Dr. Thomas Brown, honorary secretary of the Great Yarmouth Club, was explaining the new ground score concept to a friend, the friend joked that the imaginary opponent was a "regular boogey man." Some speculate that Dr. Browne's friend was influenced by a newly popular song of the time whose refrain was, "Hush! hush! hush! Here comes the bogey man."

The USGA says the song was "The Bogey Man" and later was known as "The Colonel Bogey March." However, that latter musical piece was not published until 1914, although its title is connected with one of the composer's golfing experiences. According to author Browning, during another introduction of this new fashion of scoring to the honorary secretary of another golfing club in spring 1892, it was suggested that "nothing less than the rank of Colonel would befit the dignity of a player so steady and accurate."

Other golfers picked up the term—meaning it as a compliment—and soon enough "ground score" was replaced in common usage by the word "bogey." Players then considered themselves matched against the mythical Colonel Bogey.

As golfers got better and scores started dropping early in the twentieth century, all professionals and the top amateur players began shooting scores well under the established bogey numbers still in use at most British courses. In 1911, the USGA adopted exact distances for determining what it called "par" on all holes, and suddenly bogey wasn't so good, as the meaning switched to one stroke over par.

In a slightly embarrassing snippet of history for the home of golf, Britain didn't join the move to par until 1925. Thus "bogey" became a stroke over par worldwide—a fist pump or a club slammed to the ground, depending on a player's skill level.

Q Which sport is played by hookers?

A Badminton players stroke the shuttlecock. In baseball, a pitcher can't bring the heat unless he's got a rubber. A good football team knows how to use its tight end to score. And if you have a weakness for hookers, then you probably like rugby. After all, the hooker is one of the most important players on the rugby field.

Even if you know nothing about the sport, you've probably seen a scrum—that bizarre moment in a rugby match when a bunch of players get all scrunched together into a huddle and push against each other until the ball pops out. In the center of that mass of humanity is each team's hooker, shouting instructions and trying to "hook" the ball out of the scrum to waiting teammates.

On the surface, the game seems a bit absurd, but it's immensely popular. Rugby, like soccer, has a huge international following that generally doesn't include Americans. The sport's 2007 World Cup drew an estimated 4.2 billion TV viewers worldwide.

Rugby emerged in England and got its name from Rugby School, where the first official rules of the game were established in 1845. Along the way, the sport split into two versions: rugby union and rugby league. The rules and scoring differ somewhat, and a rugby union team has fifteen players while a rugby league team has thirteen. Rugby union is the more popular version these days.

To the casual American observer, rugby looks like a variant of football: The ball is oval-shaped, the field is rectangular (though a little larger than a football gridiron) and features goalposts, and the general idea is to advance the ball across the opponent's goal line. And indeed, football is a direct descendant of rugby, which was a relatively popular sport in North America for a brief period in the late nineteenth century and again on the West Coast in the early twentieth century (the U.S. team captured Olympic gold in 1920 and 1924).

Rugby teams also rack up their points in much the same way that football teams do. In rugby union, a try (the equivalent of a touchdown) is worth five points, a conversion (a kick through the goal posts after a try, like football's extra point) is two points, and a drop goal (which resembles a field goal) is three points. The point values differ slightly in rugby league, but the basic idea is the same.

So what separates rugby players from their American counterparts? For starters, rugby players don't wear helmets, shoulder pads, or much of any protective gear at all. (We think that they may wear athletic supporters, but we are definitely not going to ask.) The sport attracts a certain adventurous type of individual—a stout, spirited character who is full of energy and fond of malt-based beverages. For this reason, you should never make hooker jokes in the presence of rugby players. Let us, cowering safely behind our keyboards, do that for you.

Q In bowling, why are three strikes in a row called a turkey?

A We love bowling. Love the mustaches, the tinted glasses, the fingerless gloves. We love that airvent thingy on the ball rack, and we love the swirling balls that are inscribed with names like Lefty and Dale. We love  the satin shirts and multicolored shoes (okay, maybe not the shoes so much). But what we love most are the terms. The Dutch 200, the

Brooklyn strike, the Cincinnati, the Jersey, the Greek Church, and especially the Turkey.

We have no idea what any of these terms mean, but we love them all the same.

Believe it or not, bowling wasn't always the sexy, hip sport played by highly trained athletes that it is today. Some historians trace bowling's roots back to 3200 B.C., while others place its origin in Europe in the third century A.D. Regardless, some form of bowling has been popular for centuries.

For much of this history, however, bowling didn't have a particularly sterling reputation. Quite the opposite: Legend holds that King Edward III banned bowling after his good-for-nothing soldiers kept skipping archery practice to roll. And well into the nineteenth century, American towns were passing laws that forbid bowling, largely because of the gambling that went along with it.

Despite these attempts at suppression—or perhaps because of them—bowling increased in popularity. In 1895, the American Bowling Congress (now known as the United States Bowling Congress) was formed, and local and regional bowling clubs began proliferating. It was around this time that the term "turkey," which signifies three strikes in a row, came into being. In an attempt to cash in on the burgeoning popularity of the newly sanctioned sport, as well as draw customers, many bowling alley proprietors offered a free live turkey to bowlers who successfully rolled three strikes in a row during Thanksgiving or Christmas week. Sadly, turkeys are no longer awarded at bowling alleys, although the tradition of shouting "turkey" when somebody manages three strikes in a row continues.

So the next time you cry "fowl" at the bowling alley, you can take pride in knowing that you're continuing a time-honored tradition. Now if we could just figure out who decided two-toned bowling shoes were a good idea, we'd really be on to something.

Who is Uncle Charlie?

A No, Uncle Charlie isn't the guy who gives you a roll of quarters for your birthday every year. In fact, when it comes to baseball, Uncle Charlie isn't a person at all—it's a nickname for the good old-fashioned pitch known as the curveball.

The legendary curveball relies on tight spin to create a sharp downward or sideward turn just as the ball reaches home plate. Many historians credit William Arthur "Candy" Cummings with inventing the popular pitch in the 1860s. As the story goes, the teenage Cummings noticed that by using certain wrist movements, he could manipulate the path of a clamshell as he flung it into the ocean. He tried these same techniques on a baseball, and after some trial and error the ball curved in the air—even when Cummings pitched underhanded, as required by the rules of baseball at the time. Cummings pitched professionally for a decade, baffling batters with his ball-busting creation.

Today, Cummings' curveball boasts many different nicknames, including the hammer, the hook, the deuce, and even the yakker. But why Uncle Charlie? Unfortunately, the answer remains shrouded in mystery. Paul Dickson's *The New Dickson Baseball Dictionary* claims the name derives from citizens band (CB) radio lingo of the 1970s; Uncle Charlie was a common nickname for the Federal Communications Commission (FCC) among CB broadcasters. How this became connected to the curveball is anyone's guess, although the accepted theory attributes it to phonetic similarities between the words "Charlie" and "curve."

Whatever its origin, Uncle Charlie remains a popular term to this day. Former major league pitcher Dwight Gooden's curve was so good, it was nicknamed Lord Charles. (Players have personified several other pitches, most notably the split-finger fastball, known to many as Mr. Splitty.) So the next time someone offers to introduce you to Uncle Charlie, don't set another place at the dinner table—put on a catcher's mitt, and keep your eye on the ball.

Q Why do golfers yell "Fore!" when they hit an errant shot?

A No one has a definite answer. There are only theories—some logical, some quite far-fetched. One theory—we'll let you decide how believable—traces it back to warnings used between artillery gunners and golfers outside a Scottish fort in the late sixteenth century.

We know that some version of the shout goes back more than a century; it turns up as common etiquette in Robert Forgan's 1881 version of *The Golfer's Handbook*. Before that, who knows?

The United States Golf Association (USGA) agrees that "fore" is Scottish in origin and suggests it's a version of a warning that meant "look out ahead" in military circles. The USGA's conclusion is that the old military term—which was used by artillery men to troops in forward positions—simply got adopted by golfers around the eighteenth century. That's one possibility.

Then there is the issue of the "forecaddie," a person who is retained to go ahead of players to mark the lies of balls in play. Here's that theory, according to the British Golf Museum: "It may be that, over time, the word forecaddie was shortened when yelled as warning to this person and the word has remained in use since."

The simplest explanation might be the one offered up by Brent Kelley in *Your Guide to Golf.* "Fore is another word for 'ahead' (think of a ship's fore and aft)," Kelley wrote. "Yelling 'fore' is simply a shorter way to yell 'watch out ahead.'"

Neil JB Laird did a thorough background search of the word "fore" in the book *Scottish Golf History,* which was published in 2003. Laird acknowledges that "...no certain etymology for the golf word 'Fore!' has been agreed." However, he proposes three possibilities:

First, that it was indeed shouted as a warning to forecaddies, who were supposed to stand as close as possible to where a shot would land. Laird points out that forecaddies originally were employed because golf balls were expensive and players didn't want to lose them.

Second, that the exclamation comes from military battles during the musket era, when various ranks would fire over the heads of their comrades. There is speculation that the word "fore" was used to warn soldiers in front to keep their heads down.

Third, that gunners might have been giving fair warning to nearby golfers. The excavation of a place called Ramsay's Fort, a sixteenth-century fortification outside Leith, Scotland, shows the fort overlooked

Leith Links, a golf course that still exists today. Laird suggests that because the people of Leith were quite well connected politically, gunners at the fort might have yelled out to them before they began firing practice—and that eventually the golfers simply picked up the term themselves.

What is cauliflower ear?

A First things first, people: If you're going to name a malady or a disease, for goodness sake, don't name it after food. It's unsettling. Some of us like to eat cauliflower, but then we come across a reference to cauliflower ear, we get a little curious, and the next thing we know, we're looking at disgusting pictures of actual human ears that, much to our dismay, really do look like cauliflower.

Because that's what happens with cauliflower ear: The ear puffs up and takes on a curdled look not unlike that of cauliflower. It can happen to anybody who suffers an injury to their outer ear; wrestlers, boxers, and martial artists who don't wear protective headgear are particularly susceptible.

Bleeding between the ear's cartilage and skin results in swelling. The skin can turn pale or purple. If cauliflower ear is not treated in a timely manner, the cartilage will be deprived of nutrients and the condition can become permanent, with little hope of returning the ear to the original shape that we all prefer to see on the sides of peoples' heads.

The remedy for cauliflower ear is fairly simple: Blood is drained from the ear and any infection is treated. Boiling, steaming, and butter are not necessary.

Q What does the term "hospital throw" mean?

A Baseball is full of fascinating jargon. A "hospital throw" refers to a throw to a base that forces the fielder to take his eye off an approaching runner. We're not quite sure where the term originated, but it is descriptive of the potential for injury. Here are some other terms to build your baseball vocabulary:

Airmail: A throw, often from the outfield, that overshoots its intended target. Origin: Descriptive.

Angler: A ballplayer who looks for endorsement opportunities. Origin: Descriptive, from fishing.

Aspirin: A baseball, particularly when thrown hard. Also: pill, pea. Origin: Descriptive. A ball resembles an aspirin when it's thrown so fast it appears to the batter to shrink.

Banjo hitter: A hitter with little power. Origin: Refers to the banjo's twangy sound and/or describes the fragile musical instrument as if it were a bat.

Barber: A talkative player. Origin: Descriptive of the stereotypical chatty barber.

Battery: The pitcher and catcher, together. Origin: Telegraphy, referring to the transmitter (pitcher) and receiver (catcher).

Bees in the hands: The "stinging" sensation that occurs after swinging the bat, particularly when not wearing protective gloves and/or in cold weather. Origin: Descriptive of stings.

Blue: An umpire. Origin: Historically, the color of their uniform.

Bullpen: Where relievers warm up. Origin: "Bull Durham" tobacco advertisements often appeared on outfield walls near the area. May also refer to an area of the park where relief pitchers gather and "shoot the bull" for long stretches of the game.

Can of corn: An easy basket catch. Origin: Refers to a grocer retrieving canned goods from high shelves by pushing them with a stick and allowing them to drop into his smock.

Catbird seat: A favorable ball-strike situation for a pitcher or a hitter. Origin: Refers to the perch of the catbird. Popularized by broadcaster Red Barber.

Cleanup hitter: The fourth batter in the lineup. Origin: He clears, or cleans, the bases occupied by the first three hitters.

Deuce: Curveball. Origin: Usually signaled for with two fingers.

Fireman: A relief pitcher, usually the ace. Origin: Descriptive.

Fungo: Fielding practice retrieving hit balls, and the special bat used to hit those practice balls. Origin: Numerous theories, ranging from a combination of the words "fun" and "go," to the cricket expression "fun goes," to the German word "fungen," or catch.

Get the thumb: To be ejected from the game. Origin: Descriptive of an umpire's hand signal.

The good face: A positive but unscientific assessment of a player's fitness, attitude, and "makeup." Origin: Scouting. A player possessing such qualities is said to have "the good face."

Jack: A home run, or to hit a home run. Origin: Descriptive of jack, meaning "to lift."

Keystone: Second base, or the second baseman. Origin: Like the keystone of an arch, second base is considered a key supporting element (for scoring runs) and a key defensive position.

Matador: A timid fielder. Origin: Bullfighting. Refers to a player who fields a ball to his side, like the movement of a bullfighter, rather than get in front of it.

O-fer or Ohfer: Going hitless over a game or other period. Origin: Puns. O-fer is "zero-for," and "ohfer" includes the exclamation "oh" as in "oh-for-5."

Ribbies: Runs batted in. Origin: Phonetic, plural pronunciation of the acronym "RBI."

Southpaw: A left-handed pitcher. Origin: In most ballparks, home plate faces east so as to keep the sun from a batter's eyes, meaning south would be on the pitcher's left side.

Stepping in the bucket: When a batter pulls away from a pitch with his front foot. Origin: Probably refers to the dugout, which often contained a bucket of water.

Tablesetter: The first and second hitters in a lineup, or a player who reaches base early in an inning. Origin: Descriptive of preparation for the cleanup hitter.

Texas Leaguer: A bloop single, similar to a dying quail or ducksnort. Origin: Named for the Texas League, where minor-leaguers of dubious skill might play.

Chapter 8
MYTHS AND TRUTHS

Q **Did Leo Durocher really coin the phrase "nice guys finish last"?**

A Long considered to be a placard for the passive and polite, the saying "Nice guys finish last" is credited to baseball manager Leo Durocher. For decades he sailed his ship on the wave created by that quote, but according to Durocher himself, he merely used the phrase best.

Known as "The Lip" during his lengthy major league career as a player and on-field manager, Leo Durocher was always quick with a quip and a colorful anecdote. On July 6, 1946, when he was bench boss of the Brooklyn Dodgers, Durocher was shooting the breeze with sports scribe Frank Graham about that afternoon's opponents, the crosstown-rival New York Giants. The Dodgers, known affectionately as "Da bums" by the Brooklyn faithful, were a motley crew of reprobates who played hard both on and off the field. When asked to describe the Giants, Durocher supposedly said: "Take a look at them. They're all nice guys, but they'll finish last. Nice guys. Finish last." In his summation of the conversation the following day, Graham shortened the quote to "Nice guys finish last."

At the time, Durocher denied making the remark, and his account of the episode was substantiated by *New York Times* pundit Lou Effrat, who was adamant that the Lip had actually lamented, "Nice guys finish eighth," referring to the number of teams in the league.

In 1992, Ralph Keyes compiled a book of misquotes titled *Nice Guys Finish Seventh*. In his version of the events, Durocher said: "Why, they're the nicest guys in the world! And where are they? In seventh place." Which is where the Giants were in the standings when the Lip started flapping. Although no one can agree on what was actually said, Durocher nonetheless titled his 1975 best-selling autobiography—what else?—*Nice Guys Finish Last*.

Q Did Sonny Liston fake a fall?

 On February 25, 1964, Sonny Liston and Muhammed Ali (then called Cassius Clay), met in Florida. Liston, the World Heavyweight Champion, started the fight as the favorite, but lost in seven rounds. The two men had a widely-publicized rematch on May 25, 1965. When Sonny Liston hit the canvas less than two minutes into their second heavyweight-belt bout, pundits immediately accused the former champ of taking a dive. Did the lumbering Liston really fake a fall?

Even without the controversial conclusion to the widely publicized rematch, there was enough ink and intrigue to fill a John LeCarre spy novel. The bout against Ali—who had just joined the Nation of Islam and changed his name from Cassius Clay—was held in a 6,000-seat arena in Lewiston, Maine, after numerous states refused to sanction the fight because of militant behavior associated with the Muslim movement. Robert Goulet, the velvet-voiced crooner entrust-

ed with singing the national anthem, forgot the words to the song, and the third man in the ring, Jersey Joe Walcott, was a former heavyweight champion but a novice referee.

One minute and 42 seconds into the fight, Ali threw a quick upper-cut that seemed to connect with nothing but air. Liston tumbled to the tarmac, though no one seemed sure whether it was the breeze from the blow or the blow itself that put him there. Liston was ulti-mately counted out by the ringside timer, not the in-ring referee.

Since it was a largely invisible swing (dubbed the "phantom punch" by sports scribes) that floored Liston, he was accused of cashing it in just to cash in. Evidence proves otherwise. Film footage of the bout shows Liston caught flush with a quick, pistonlike "anchor" punch that Ali claimed was designed to be a surprise. Liston actu-ally got back up and was trading body blows with the Louisville Lip when the referee stepped in, stopped the fight, and informed Liston that his bid to become the first boxer to regain the heavyweight title was over.

Q Is the Heisman Trophy cursed?

A After being named best college football player in the nation, one's best position might be "fallback." Those who believe the Heisman Curse is just a sports myth should consider the following facts.

During a football game in 1934, University of Chicago running back Jay Berwanger collided with University of Michigan defender Gerald Ford, bloodying the tackler's left cheek. The resulting scar on the future U.S. president would be permanent—as would, some say, the so-called Heisman Curse it begat.

A year later, Berwanger was awarded the first Heisman Trophy, emblematic of the best player in college football. Although he also became the first man ever drafted by the NFL, the "Genius of the Gridiron" never played another snap. In fact, surprisingly few of the six dozen trophy recipients since have made more of an impact.

In recent years, the list of Heisman honorees has included several pro football busts, especially at the marquee quarterback position. Charlie Ward (1993), Eric Crouch (2001), and Jason White (2003) never played an NFL game. Danny Wuerffel (1996) earned just ten starts, and though Chris Weinke (2000) made 19, his team won just one of them.

Berwanger himself tacitly acknowledged that the Heisman wasn't worth the 25 pounds of bronze used to cast it. Until he eventually donated it to his alma mater, the trophy was displayed in his aunt's library—as a doorstop.

Q Can a sports game have an effect on a city's sewage system?

A Every year at the end of January, rumors begin to swirl that the sewer systems in several major cities fail due to the number of toilets that are flushed during halftime of the Super Bowl. But are the rumors true?

During Super Bowl XVIII in 1984, a water main in Salt Lake City ruptured, dampening the sporting spirit in that community. The next day, conversations around office water coolers were rife with rumors that toilet trauma, prompted by a flood of beverage-logged football fans all using the facilities at the same time, had caused the sewer systems of numerous cities to clog up.

Such a myth would almost make sense if it were applied to the final of the World Cup of soccer, where there is continuous action without stoppages of any kind until the halftime break. But anyone who has sat through the six-plus-hour spectacle known as the Super Bowl realizes that there is no merit to this tall tale. The North American brand of football—especially the game played on that particular Sunday—has numerous breaks, pauses, and lapses throughout. So to suggest there is a simultaneous dash to the latrine at any time during this all-day marathon is silly.

Not only that, but the quality of Super Bowl TV commercials (which cost millions for a 30-second spot) usually keeps even disinterested viewers glued to their seats. Although the ads aired on Super Bowl Sunday are among the most highly anticipated events in that day's lineup, most of them are shown during the pre-game, halftime, and post-game spectacles, leaving valuable lulls during football action for human nature's pause for the cause.

Can you really break a concrete block with your hand?

A It's an act that's synonymous with martial arts, and it's not just a Hollywood invention. Here we'll reveal some of the tricks of the concrete-busting trade.

In a face-off between hand and block, the hand has a surprising advantage: Bone is significantly stronger than concrete. In fact, bone can withstand about 40 times more stress than concrete before reaching its breaking point. What's more, the surrounding muscles and ligaments in your hands are good stress absorbers, making the hand and arm one tough weapon. So if you position your hand correctly, you're not going to break it by hitting a block of concrete.

The trick to smashing a block is thrusting this sturdy mass into the concrete with enough force to bend the block beyond its breaking point. The force of any impact is determined by the momentum of the two objects in the collision. Momentum is a multiple of the mass and velocity of an object.

Velocity is the key. When striking an object, the speed of your blow is critical. You also have to hit the block with a relatively small area of your hand, so that the force of the impact is focused in one spot on the block—this concentrates the stress on the concrete. As in golf, the only way for a martial arts student to hit accurately with greater speed is practice, practice, practice.

But there is a basic mental trick involved: You have to overcome your natural instinct to slow your strike as your hand approaches the block. Martial arts masters concentrate on an impact spot beyond the block, so that the hand is still at maximum speed when it makes contact with the concrete.

You also need to put as much body mass as you can into the strike; this can be achieved by twisting your body and lowering your torso as you make contact. A black belt in karate can throw a chop at about 46 feet per second, which results in a force of about 2,800 newtons. (A newton is the unit of force needed to accelerate a mass.)

That's more than enough power to break the standard one-and-a-half-inch concrete slabs that are commonly used in demonstrations and typically can withstand only 1,900 newtons. Nonetheless, while hands are dandy in a block-breaking exhibition, you'll find that for sidewalk demolition and other large projects, jackhammers are really the way to go.

Did Knute Rockne really ask his team to "Win one for the Gipper"?

A Sorry, but you'll have to credit Hollywood, not Notre Dame football coach Knute Rockne, with the emotional plea.

The oft-repeated line is from the movie *Knute Rockne: All American*, which was released in 1940. In the famous football flick, Rockne tells his troops that their teammate George Gipp's dying words were: "Rock, sometime when the team is up against it and the breaks are beating the boys, tell them to go out there with all they've got and win just one for the Gipper." No one really knows what Gipp and his coach talked about in the days before the star player's death. Gipp died in 1920 of an infection from strep throat, and Rockne met his own tragic fate in a plane crash in 1931, so neither man was in a position to refute the scriptwriter's soliloquy.

What is known is this: Rockne didn't get around to using Gipp's request as a motivating muscle until 1928, a full eight years after George died. According to Francis Wallace, the newspaper reporter who was responsible for dubbing the team the "Fighting Irish," Rockne made his famous speech to his underdog charges before a game against Army at Yankee Stadium on November 10, 1928. Wallace reported that Rockne rose before the assembled throng and said, "The day before he died, George Gipp asked me to wait until the situation seemed hopeless and then ask a Notre Dame team to go out and beat Army for him. This is the day, and you are the team." Although that does evoke the spirit of "win one for the Gipper," in reality those words are a Hollywood embellishment.

The quote gained new life when Ronald Reagan, who played the role of Gipp in the Hollywood homily about Rockne, used the catchphrase as a rallying cry during the 1988 Republican Convention.

Q Is the gambling industry rigged in favor of the house?

A Remember those ads that said, "What Happens in Vegas Stays in Vegas"? The ones that seemed to suggest that there are hordes of jaw-droppingly beautiful women who can't wait to get to Sin City and hook up with complete strangers? Here's a little secret: Those advertisements may not have been 100 percent accurate.

You see, the folks who own the casinos in Las Vegas are always looking for ways to lure you there. Because they know that once you arrive and figure out that the eager supermodel quotient isn't nearly as high as the creepy-guys-looking-for-supermodels quotient (not to mention the chain-smoking-senior-citizen quotient), you'll shrug your shoulders and find something else to do.

Namely, gambling. And then they've got you. The beauty of Las Vegas (and we mean the beauty from the casino owners' perspective, not the stunning beauty of the fake Eiffel Tower or the fake Venetian canals) is that the games don't have to be rigged in favor of the house—they're set up in favor of the house, openly and legally.

Casino owners carefully study the probable outcomes of their games and then design the rules so that the house will win a certain small percentage over the long haul. Government bodies like the Nevada Gaming Commission regulate these house advantages and work to ensure that the casinos stick to them. If the house advantage on a game is 5 percent, that means the casino will pocket about 5 percent of all the money gambled, returning the other 95 percent to the players.

But the returned money is distributed unequally—many gamblers will have small losses or gains while a few will win (or lose) big. And the possibility of becoming a big winner is what keeps you going, in spite of the fact that in the long term, when all things are considered, the house always wins.

The percentages vary by game, but they can exceed 10 percent in some cases. If you study the rules of blackjack, for example, and learn how to play it skillfully, you'll have better odds of winning than if you drop all your dough into a slot machine, which is typically your worst bet. Nevertheless, even blackjack favors the house. So, yes, the gambling industry is set up so that the casino owner makes a profit. What, you thought fake Eiffel Towers grow on trees?

Q Did Babe Ruth call his shot in the 1932 World Series?

A Most of Babe Ruth's achievements can be appraised by statistics, but a prominent one is stuck in the vortex between fact and fantasy.

Like the conundrum about whether those flailing arms in the distant ocean signal waving or drowning, Babe Ruth's finger to the sky in Game 3 of the 1932 World Series must be interpreted by the eye of the beholder.

The Bambino hated the Chicago Cubs, whose fans had been pelting him with trash and whose players' taunts infuriated him. So when Ruth came to the plate in the fifth inning with the score tied 4–4, he seemed to mock his nemeses when he lifted his index finger and pointed...somewhere.

Although conventional wisdom credits the great slugger with indicating that Charlie Root's next pitch was destined for Wrigley Field's centerfield bleachers, most onlookers later recounted that Ruth appeared to point to the pitcher...or to the Cubs' dugout...or perhaps that he was simply indicating the count.

There's no debating what happened next: Ruth hammered a 440-foot laser over the wall, getting his Yankees back into the game and propelling them to an eventual four-game sweep.

Subsequent news stories nurtured the notion that the Babe "called" his shot. Many of the principals begged to differ. "He [just] indicated he had one more strike remaining," assessed Frank Crosetti, Babe's teammate. Former major leaguer Babe Herman even claimed to have overheard a conversation between Root and Ruth years later in which the hitter said, "I know I didn't [call it]. But it made a hell of a story, didn't it?"

In 2000, ESPN aired a newly unearthed 16 mm film of the episode, which, though not definitive, indicated that Ruth was merely gesturing to Chicago's bench.

Whether called or merely mauled, the shot was the last of the Sultan of Swat's 15 World Series home runs.

Chapter 9
THE OLYMPIC GAMES

Q **What were the ancient Olympic Games like?**

A Imagine attending a sporting event where blood and broken limbs are the norm. It's hot out but water is scarce; the food is overpriced and lousy. Motels are few, pricey, and crummy. Almost everyone has to camp out. Your bleacher seat feels like freshly heated limestone. Forty thousand drunken, screaming savages surround you.

No, you aren't at a modern Division I-A college football game hosted by an eastern Washington agricultural university. You're at the ancient Greek Olympic Games! Millennia later, nations will suspend the Games in wartime; for these Olympics, Greek nations will (for the most part) suspend wartime.

The games took place in Olympia, which was a remote, scenic religious sanctuary in the western Greek boonies. The nearest town was little Elis, 40 miles away. According to chroniclers, the ancient Olympic Games started in 776 B.C. That's about a century after Elijah and Jezebel's biblical difference of opinion. Rome wasn't yet founded; the Assyrian Empire ruled the Near East. Greece's fractious city-states waged constant political and military struggle. In 776, with disease and strife even worse than usual in Greece, King Iphitos of Elis consulted the Delphic Oracle. She said, roughly translated: "Greece is cursed. Hold athletics at Olympia, like you guys used to do, to lift the curse."

"Done deal," said the king. Greek legend spoke of games of old held at Olympia in honor of Zeus, occurring perhaps every four or five years, so Iphitos cleared some land at Olympia and put on a footrace. The plague soon petered out. "Wish it was always that easy," Iphitos probably said.

It's uncertain why the Eleans decided to repeat the Olympics every four years; that was probably the most prevalent version of the ancient tradition. Likely, they lacked the resources to do it more often. Whatever the reason, the Games became Elis's reason for being. Its people spent the intervening years preparing for the next Olympiad. Given the amount of feasting and drinking that happened at the Games, the first year was likely spent recuperating and rebuilding.

Over the centuries, the event program extended to five days. The Eleans added equestrian and combat events. Any male Greek athlete could try out for the Games. Winners became rock stars, with egos and fringe benefits to match. There were no silver or bronze medals; losers slunk away in shame.

Temples and facilities sprang up at Olympia over the years: a great arena, shrines, and training facilities. Historians believe that in the lengthy heyday of the games, 40,000-plus people would converge on Olympia to see a sport program ranging from chariot racing to track-and-field events to hand-to-hand combat.

And athletes weren't the only ones who competed—artists and writers could compete in cultural events as well. Records are scarce, but the writer Herodotus was one participant. Competing in 444 B.C. at Olympia, Greece, the athlete participated in both writing and sporting contests. His pairing of brains and brawn would represent the ideal throughout much of the ancient era. (In a nod to that ancient tradition, the modern Games held artistic competitions in such events as architecture, painting, sculpture, music, and literature between 1912 and 1948).

Except for the boxers, wrestlers, charioteers, and pankratists (freestyle fighters)— who were frequently maimed or killed—the athletes had it easy compared to the attendees. The climate was hot and sticky, without even a permanent water source for most of the ancient Olympic era (a rich guy finally built an aqueduct). Deaths from sunstroke weren't rare. Sanitation? Most people had no way to bathe, so everyone stank, and disease ran rampant.

Married women couldn't attend, except female owners of racing chariots. The only other exception was a priestess of Demeter, who had her own special seat. Unmarried girls and women, especially prostitutes, were welcome. According to historians and pottery depictions, athletes competed nude, so there was no chance a woman could infiltrate as a competitor.

For five days every four years, Olympia combined the features of church, carnival, track meet, martial arts, banquet, racing, bachelor party, brothel, and tourist trap into a Woodstock-like scene of organized bedlam. The Olympics weren't merely to be watched or even experienced. They were to be endured and survived.

In A.D. 393, Roman Emperor Theodosius I, a first-rank killjoy, banned all pagan ceremonies. Since the Games' central ritual was a big sacrifice to Zeus, this huge heathen debauch clearly had to go.

The party was over. It wouldn't start again for centuries.

Q Which country was the first after Greece to host the Olympic Games?

A The first modern Olympic Games under the auspices of the International Olympic Committee were held in Athens in 1896, although there were preceding events in Greece as far back as 1859. The second modern Olympic Games were held in 1900 in Paris and were billed as part of the Exposition Universelle Internationale, the world's fair that featured the unveiling of the Eiffel Tower. It was the first Olympiad to be held outside of Greece, and there were plenty of other firsts to it as well.

1. Despite the fact that almost a thousand athletes competed in the 1900 Olympics, spectator attendance was low. The press preferred to focus on the Paris Exposition and seldom referred to the games as actual Olympic events. Instead, they were reported variously as "International Championships," "Paris Championships," "World Championships," and even "Grand Prix of the Paris Exposition." The founder of the International Olympic Committee, Baron Pierre de Coubertin, later said: "It's a miracle that the Olympic movement survived that celebration."

2. The Olympic status of the athletes was equally downplayed, to the extent that many competitors never actually knew they were participating in the Olympics. Margaret Ives Abbott, a student of art from Chicago who won the nine-hole women's golf tournament, died in 1955 without realizing she was America's first female Olympic champion.

3. Because the Olympics were held in conjunction with the Paris Exhibition, the scheduling and locations of the sporting events were often absurd. The fencing competition, for instance, was held as a sort of sideshow in the exhibition's cutlery area, and swimmers were forced to battle the polluted waters and strong currents of the Seine.

4. After preliminary rounds, Myer Prinstein (from Syracuse University) had a clear lead in the long-jump competition and seemed poised to win. But when the final jump was scheduled on a Sunday, the official in charge of U.S. athletes disapproved of their competing on the Christian Sabbath. The athletes gave their word not to participate; Prinstein, who was Jewish, reluctantly agreed as well. On Sunday, however, Prinstein's main rival, Alvin Kraenzlein (University of Pennsylvania), broke his promise and competed, beating Prinstein's qualifying jump by a centimeter and winning the gold. Allegedly, Prinstein was so angry that he punched Kraenzlein in the face.

5. Alvin Kraenzlein also won the 110-meter hurdles, the 220-meter hurdles, and the 60-meter dash—all in three days. As of 2012, he was still the only track-and-field athlete to have won four gold medals in individual events at a single Olympics.

6. Women made their first appearance in the 1900 Games, albeit in small numbers: Of the thousand or so athletes participating, only 22 were women. The first female Olympic champion was Charlotte

Cooper of Great Britain, who won the tennis singles and the mixed doubles. Female athletes wore the ankle-length skirts and dresses typical of the time.

7. Ray Ewry of Indiana won the gold in three championships—standing high jump, standing long jump, and standing triple jump—all on the same day. A remarkable feat for any man, these victories amounted to Olympic heroism for Ewry, who had spent his childhood confined to a wheelchair because of polio.

8. After the French won both gold and silver medals in the marathon, three runners from the United States contested the results, accusing the winners of taking a short cut. As proof, they submitted their observation that the new champions were the only contestants not splattered with mud. Although the objection was not sustained, the celebratory spirit had been soured.

9. The 1900 Olympics saw the Games' youngest champion. On August 26, two Dutch rowers suddenly needed a replacement coxswain and chose a French boy, undoubtedly because of his small size. The pair rowed to a close victory, and the boy joined them in the victory ceremony. He then disappeared, but a photograph taken of the boy and the rowers indicates that he could have been as young as ten years old.

Q Who was the first Olympic champion in the modern games?

A If today's television coverage had existed in the times of American athlete James Connolly, producers could have put together a pretty slick profile piece on Connolly and his route to the Olympic Games. Connolly was 27 years old when he competed in the 1896 Games in Athens, and his story was a compelling one. We love athletes who came from humble beginnings; James Connolly grew up playing rough-and-tumble games in the streets of Boston, as one of twelve children born to poor Irish immigrants. We love self-made men, and Connolly, who dropped out of high school as a boy, fit the bill when he later pursued a course of self-education that earned him admission to Harvard. We love people who sacrifice for their sport, and Connolly did so, when he had to withdraw from Harvard in order to pursue his dream of competing in the Olympics.

Fortunately, Connolly's sacrifice was not in vain. He won the first medal awarded in the Games (and a place in the Olympic history books) in the "hop-step-jump" competition—what we now call the triple jump—against a field of seven competitors. Measuring a distance of 13.71 meters, his jump beat that of the French competitor who won second place, Alexandre Tufferi, by a full meter.

Connolly didn't take home gold, though, but silver. That's because in 1896, a silver medal was given for the top spot and bronze for second place, while the poor third-place finisher went home empty-handed. Later, the International Olympic Committee retroactively assigned gold, silver, and bronze medals to the top three competitors in each event according to modern rules. So for the history books, Connolly's medal count in the 1896 Games stands at three: his gold for the triple jump, a silver for second place in the high jump, and a bronze for third place in the long jump.

Connolly also competed in the 1900 Olympic Games in Paris, where he added one more medal to his count, again in the Triple Jump. Although he exceeded his past Olympic performance with a distance of 13.97 meters, he came in second place, behind his U.S. teammate Meyer Prinstein's winning distance of 14.41 meters.

Connolly went on to become a successful journalist and novelist, specializing in maritime writing.

Q What has kept athletes from competing in the Olympic Games?

A After years of training, even Olympic-caliber athletes are vulnerable to last-minute injuries that dash their hopes. Athletes are sidelined by everything from the common pulled muscle or cold to more unexpected ailments. For instance, in 1912 Sweden's cyclist Carl Landsberg was hit by a motor wagon during a road race and was dragged down the road. The performance of runners Pekka Vasala (Finland) and Silvio Leonard (Cuba) suffered in 1968 and 1976 when Vasala got Montezuma's Revenge and Leonard cut his foot on a cologne bottle. Perhaps the most memorable Olympic disaster was when Janos Baranyai of Hungary dislocated his elbow while lifting 148 kg during the 2008 Beijing Olympics. Who knew the Olympics could be so dangerous? Here are more examples from over the years:

1906: Runner Harvey Cohn was almost swept overboard, and six athletes required medical treatment, when the *SS Barbarossa* was hit by a large wave enroute to Athens. Several favored U.S. athletes did poorly or dropped out because of their "ocean adventure."

1912: Francisco Lazaro of Portugal collapsed during the marathon and died the next day from sunstroke.

1936: After losing his opening round at the Berlin Olympics, Thomas Hamilton-Brown, a lightweight boxer from South Africa, drowned his sorrows with food. But the competitors' scores had accidentally been switched. Sadly, the damage was done—a five-pound weight gain kept Hamilton-Brown from the final round.

1948: Shortly after arriving in London, Czech gymnast Eliska Misakova was hospitalized. She died of infantile paralysis the day her team competed and won the gold. At the award ceremony, the Czech flag was bordered in black.

1960: During the cycling road race in Rome, Dane Knut Jensen suffered sunstroke, fractured his skull in a fall, and died.

1960: Wym Essajas, Suriname's sole athlete, misunderstood the schedule and missed his 800-meter race. Suriname couldn't send another athlete to the Olympics until 1972.

1964: Australian skier Ross Milne died during a practice run for the men's downhill at Innsbruck after smashing into a tree.

1968: Mexico City's altitude of 7,347 feet slowed the times of endurance events in the 1968 games. Three men running the 10,000-meter were unable to finish while others fell unconscious at the finish line.

1972: The Munich Massacre of 1972 resulted in the deaths of eleven Israeli athletes, five Palestinian terrorists, and one German policeman after the kidnapping of the athletes.

1972: U.S. runners Eddie Hart, Rey Robinson, and Robert Taylor, supplied with an outdated schedule, rushed to the 100-meter semifinals at the last minute. Hart and Robinson, both winners in the quarterfinals, missed their heats. Taylor ran and won the silver medal.

1972: Sixteen-year-old swimmer Rick DeMont took two Marex pills for an asthma attack the day before his 400-meter freestyle race. His gold medal was revoked when he failed the drug test. The team physicians never checked to see whether his prescription contained banned substances. The same thing happened to Romanian gymnast Andreea Raducan in 2000. She was stripped of her gold medal for the all-around competition when she tested positive for the banned substance pseudoephedrine—an ingredient in the cold medicine provided by team doctors.

1996: Two people were killed and 111 were injured when American Eric Robert Rudolph detonated a bomb at the Atlanta Olympics.

2010: During the 2010 Winter Olympics in Vancouver, Georgian luger Nodar Kumaritashvili died during a training run on the luge track, losing control of his sled in a tight turn and crashing headlong into a steel support pole. Kumaritashvili's death prompted officials to alter the luge course in an attempt to make it less dangerous. Sadly, the modifications came too late for Nodar.

Who was the oldest Olympic medalist?

Think of the average Olympic athlete, and the following images likely come to mind: physical perfection, drive, determination—and youth? Not necessarily. It could be just a matter of time before the AARP holds its own Olympic trials. Here are the stories behind the oldest medallists.

Hilde Pedersen: When Norway's Pedersen took home the bronze in the ten-kilometer cross-country-skiing event at the 2006 Turin Winter Olympics, she became the oldest woman to win a Winter Games Olympic medal. It was an impressive achievement for the 41-year-old, but as she and other "older" competitors have proved in the past, age is no barrier to claiming an Olympic medal.

Oscar Swahn: Swedish shooter Swahn participated in three Olympic Games. At age 60, he won two gold medals and a bronze at his first Olympics, which took place in London in 1908. Four years later, at the Sweden Games, he won a gold in the single shot running deer team, making him the world's oldest gold medalist. Swahn returned to the Olympics in 1920 at age 72 and managed to win a silver medal in the double shot running deer competition.

Anders Haugen: Even at the ripe age of 72, Swahn is not the oldest person to have won an Olympic medal. At the first Winter Olympic Games in Chamonix, France (1924), U.S. ski jumper Anders Haugen placed fourth with a score of 17.916 points. Third-place winner, Norway's Thorlief Haug, received a score of 18.000 points. Fifty years later, a sports historian determined that Haug's score had been miscalculated and that he should have finished behind Haugen. At a special ceremony in Oslo, Haugen was finally awarded the bronze medal when he was 83 years old, making him the "eldest" recipient of an Olympic medal and the only American to ever win a medal in the ski-jump event.

Q In the 1936 Olympics, which American won the gold medal in the 800-meter race?

A When we think of runners in the 1936 Olympic Games held in Berlin during the time of Nazi Germany, we inevitably think of the historic performance of Jesse Owens. Owens won gold in the 100-meter, 200-meter, and 4x100-meter relay races, as well as the long jump. He wasn't the only African-American athlete to win gold, though. Both the 400- and 800-meter events were won by Owens' teammates, Archie Williams and John Woodruff.

Californian Archie Williams won the 400-meter event. In 1936, Williams was having a very good year. Not only had he broken the 49-second barrier for the first time that year, but he set a world record at the NCAA Championships. In Berlin, he won in 46.5 seconds, closely trailed by Brit Godfrey Brown (46.7 seconds) and American James Ellis LuValle (46.8 seconds).

Williams went home to graduate from U.C. Berkeley. He later served in the military, a stint that included time as a pilot in World War II. After his retirement from the Air Force, he taught mathematics to high school students.

Woodruff, a grandson of former Virginia slaves, was born in Connellsville, Pennsylvania, in 1915. He earned national recognition in high school by running 880 yards in 1:55.1 twice in one week. This feat led to a scholarship offer from the University of Pittsburgh. Woodruff had not planned to attend college, but when he went to apply for jobs after high school, he found only racist rebuffs. Woodruff headed for Pittsburgh—the first in his family to attend college.

After arriving in Pittsburgh, Woodruff competed with the track team, but when other schools refused to compete against blacks, he stayed behind in Pittsburgh. Woodruff earned money by working on the campus grounds and cleaning the football stadium after games. He completed his freshman year of college before heading to the Berlin Olympics.

Woodruff's 800-meter race at Berlin started off badly. He became boxed in by other runners, and he came to an almost dead stop in the confusion. These circumstances, however, allowed him room to get to the outside of the pack. Once there, Woodruff blew past the other runners. The result was a thrilling come-from-behind victory— and a gold medal.

Like Williams, Woodruff joined the army after college. He fought in World War II and Korea and rose to the rank of lieutenant colonel. After his retirement from the military, he settled in New York and went into coaching and officiating.

How did the biathlon become an Olympic event?

A It's one thing to ski through the frozen countryside for a few kilometers; it's quite another to interrupt that heart-pounding exertion and muster up the calm and concentration needed to hit a target that's a few centimeters wide with a .22 caliber bolt-action rifle.

Yes, the biathlon is an odd sport. Cross-country skiing combined with rifle marksmanship? Why not curling and long jump? Figure skating and weight lifting? Snowboard and luge? (Hmm, we think we might be on to something with that last one.) In actuality, however, the two skills that make up the biathlon have a history of going hand in hand, so combining them as an Olympic event makes perfect sense.

It's no surprise that the inspiration for the biathlon came from the frigid wastes of northern Europe, where there's not much to do in the winter besides ski around and drink aquavit. Cross-country skiing provided a quick and efficient way to travel over the snowy ground, so northern cultures mastered the technique early—and it was especially useful when it came time to hunt for winter food. People on skis were killing deer with bows and arrows long before such an activity was considered a sport.

But skiing and shooting (eventually, with guns) evolved from an act of survival into a competition. The earliest biathlon competitions were held in 1767 as informal contests between Swedish and Norwegian border patrols. The sport spread through Scandinavia in the nineteenth century as sharpshooting skiers formed biathlon clubs. In 1924, it was included as a demonstration sport in the Winter Olympics in Chamonix, France, although it was called military patrol.

In 1948, the Union Internationale de Pentathlon Moderne et Biathlon—the first international governing body for the sport—was formed. The official rules for what would come to be the modern biathlon were determined over the next several years.

During the 1960 Olympics at Squaw Valley Ski Resort in California, a biathlon was contested as an official Olympic event for the first time. The sport has evolved over the decades—it now features smaller-caliber rifles, different distances, various types of relays, and the participation of women. (A women's biathlon was first staged as an Olympic event in 1992 in Albertville, France. The 2014 Games in Sochi saw the first mixed relay team.)

Today, biathlon clubs and organizations are active all over the world, and there are versions of the sport for summertime in which running replaces skiing. Still, the biathlon's popularity remains strongest in its European birthplace.

Q Does buzkashi have any chance of becoming an Olympic sport?

A Imagine a game in which the "ball" is the carcass of a goat, decapitated, dehoofed, and soaked overnight in cold water to make it stiff. The players are mounted on horseback and wear traditional Uzbek garb: turbans, robes, and scarves around their waists. There's no complicated playbook, only a minimally regimented strategy that requires—encourages—no-holds-barred violence. The referees carry rifles, in case things really get out of hand. The field has no set boundaries; spectators are in constant danger of being trampled. The objective is to gain possession of the goat and carry it to a designated goal. And the winning players cook and eat the carcass.

This is buzkashi, the national sport of Afghanistan. Buzkashi translates to "goat pulling" and likely evolved from ordinary herding. It originated with nomadic Turkic peoples who moved west from China and Mongolia from the tenth to fifteenth centuries. Today, it's played mainly in Afghanistan, but you can also find folks yanking the ol' carcass in northwestern China and in the Muslim republics north of Afghanistan.

The game has two basic forms: modern and traditional. The modern involves teams of ten to twelve riders. In the traditional form, it's every man for himself. Both require a combination of strength and expert horsemanship. The best players are generally over the age of forty, and their mounts are trained for up to five years before entering a match.

There's typically more at stake in a tournament than a tasty repast of pulled goat. The competitions often are sponsored by *khans* ("traditional elites") who gain or lose status based on the success of the events. And in this case, success is defined by how little or how much mayhem erupts. Biting, hair-pulling, grabbing another rider's reins, and using weapons are prohibited in buzkashi. Pretty much anything else goes.

Could it become an Olympic sport? Don't count on it. Then again, in a world in which millions of people tune in each week to watch socially inept twenty-somethings eat insects for fun, fame, and prizes, is barbarous goat-pulling all that far-fetched?

Chapter 10

FEATS AND FACTS FOR THE HISTORY BOOKS

Q **What year saw the Pro Football Hall of Fame induct its first group of honorees?**

A The Pro Football Hall of Fame, based in Canton, Ohio, inducted its first group of honorees on September 7, 1963. The men who earned this honor were:

Sammy Baugh: Baugh, a quarterback with the Washington Redskins, was primarily responsible for the development of the forward pass into a major offensive weapon; he threw with stunning accuracy during his career.

Bert Bell: A part-owner of first the Philadelphia Eagles and later the Pittsburgh Steelers, Bell served as commissioner of the NFL from 1945 until he passed away in 1959.

Joe Carr: Carr acted as the president of the National Football League for 18 years from 1921 to 1939. In fact, he helped to organize the National Football League, first known as the American Professional Football Association.

Earl "Dutch" Clark: Clark was inducted in the College Football Hall of Fame before being inducted in the Pro Football Hall of Fame. Professionally, he played for the Portsmouth Spartans, who then became the Detroit Lions. When his playing days were over, he served as coach to the Cleveland Rams.

Harold "Red" Grange: "Red" wasn't Grange's only nickname; he was also called "The Galloping Ghost." Grange brought his college football talents to the Chicago Bears, although he also briefly played for the New York Yankees, a team in the short-lived American Football League.

George Halas: George Halas was owner, coach, and (during the 1920s) player for the Chicago Bears and its earlier incarnations, the Decatur Staleys and the Chicago Staleys. He coached the Chicago Bears through 40 seasons (1920–1929, 1933–1942, 1946–1955, 1958–1967) and six NFL titles. At one point, he held a record 324 coaching wins (later broken by Don Shula).

Mel Hein: Hein played for the New York Giants for 15 seasons, serving at team captain for 10 seasons. In 1938, he was named the NFL's MVP during the Giant's championship season.

Wilbur "Pete" Henry: Henry played for the Canton Bulldogs, the New York Giants, and the Pottsville Maroons. He signed with the Canton Bulldogs on the same day the American Professional Football Association (later the NFL) was being organized in Canton. He contributed to the Bulldogs winning the championships in both 1922 and 1923.

Robert "Cal" Hubbard: Hubbard played for the New York Giants, Green Bay Packers, and the Pittsburgh Pirates. He was named the NFL's all-time offensive tackle in 1969. Hubbard had a second career in sports as well—he served as a baseball umpire. In fact, he's a member of the Baseball Hall of Fame!

Don Hutson: Hutson, who played for the Green Bay Packers, held a long-standing record of 99 career touchdown receptions; when he retired, he had over 488 career receptions. He was named MVP in both 1941 and 1942.

Earl "Curly" Lambeau: Lambeau was a Green Bay Packer, through and through. He was one of their founders, played on the team, and led them to six championships as a coach.

Tim Mara: Tim Mara founded the New York Giants, bringing national attention to the fledgling National Football League. His family has stayed involved with the Giants, and his son Wellington also made it into the Pro Football Hall of Fame.

George Preston Marshall: Marshall founded the Washington Redskins and acted as their owner until his death in 1969. Marshall, a showman, was influential in introducing halftime shows and marching bands to professional football.

John "Blood" McNally: McNally, a fast and flashy running back, played on five different NFL teams. He was on four NFL championship teams in his years with the Green Bay Packers.

Bronko Nagurski: Powerful fullback Bronko Nagurski played for the Chicago Bears in the 1930s, where he helped the team win two championships. Nagurski was also a professional wrestler. In 1943, Nagurski returned to the Bears, short of players due to war, and helped them win another championship.

Ernie Nevers: Nevers, a good all-around athlete, played both baseball and football professionally. He joined with the Chicago Cardinals in 1929, where in one game against the rival Chicago Bears, he famously scored 40 points.

Jim Thorpe: Considered among the greatest American athletes of all time, Thorpe achieved world prominence by blowing away the field in the pentathlon and decathlon events at the 1912 Games in Stockholm, Sweden. When it was revealed Thorpe had played semipro baseball for pay prior to the Olympics, his medals were stripped (they were reinstated after his death). But the scandal called attention to Thorpe's baseball skills, and he was subsequently signed to a contract by the New York Giants. He played outfield for three teams over six seasons, ending in 1919. At the same time, Thorpe was a magnificent fullback for pre-NFL teams and the first president—and superstar—of what would become the NFL, playing for six different teams until 1928.

Q Which hockey player has spent the most time in the penalty box?

A Oh, the stories that penalty boxes could tell...for the first 50 years of the National Hockey League's existence, every league arena had only one penalty box, which meant that players who engaged in a lively tussle on the ice served their penance together, with only an obviously nervous league official sitting between them to act as a buffer. Quite often, the combatants would continue their fisted arguments off the ice and inside their temporary, cramped quarters.

On one occasion, this led to the infamous "pickling" of New York Rangers' forward Bob Dill. On December 17, 1944, Dill and

Montreal Canadiens fireball Maurice "The Rocket" Richard engaged in a raucous set-to that banished them both to the shower stall of shame. Inside the box, the obviously dazed and confused Dill attacked The Rocket again and received another sound thumping for his lack of common sense.

It wasn't until midway through the 1963–1964 season that the league introduced a rule requiring every rink to have separate penalty benches. A particularly vicious confrontation between Toronto Maple Leaf Bob Pulford and Montreal Canadien Terry Harper on October 30, 1963, precipitated by Harper's questioning of Pulford's sexual preference, spearheaded the NHL's decision to arrive at a sensible solution.

The undisputed king of the sin bin was Dave "Tiger" Williams, who logged nearly 4,000 minutes sitting on his punitive throne during his 15-year career in the NHL. Having spent his formative years with the Toronto Maple Leafs, Williams had a personal affinity for the Maple Leaf Gardens' penalty box, which he described as "a gross place to go. The guys in there are bleeding…and no one's cleaned the place since 1938."

Williams may hold the career mark for sin bin occupancy, but the rap sheet for a single-season sentence belongs to Dave "The Hammer" Schultz. During the 1974–1975 campaign, the Philadelphia Flyers enforcer cooled his carcass in the hotel of humility for 472 minutes, nearly 8 full games. He was so at home in the house, he actually recorded a single titled "The Penalty Box," which became something of a cult hit in and around the City of Brotherly Love.

Philadelphia's post of punition was also the scene of one of hockey's most hilarious highlights. During a game between the Flyers and Maple Leafs in 2001, Toronto tough guy Tie Domi was sent to the box. Upon his arrival in the cage, he was verbally accosted by a leather-lunged Philly fan named Chris Falcone, who wisely used the glass partition to shield himself from Domi. Known as "The Albanian Assassin," Domi responded to the goading by spraying his heckler with water. The broad-shouldered Falcone lunged toward Domi, fell over the glass, and landed in a heap at Domi's feet, which resulted in a comic wrestling match between lug head and lunatic.

How many Gordie Howe Hat Tracks did Gordie Howe achieve?

One might logically assume that NHL great Gordie Howe invented the "Gordie Howe Hat Trick." Then again, when you assume...

Mr. Hockey did not invent the three-pronged feat that bears his name. In fact, the term used to describe the art of recording a goal, an assist, and a fight in a single hockey match didn't enter the sport's lexicon until 1991. That's a full ten years after the game's longest-serving veteran hung up his blades. (Howe holds the record of oldest player in the NHL—when he retired in 1980, he was 52 years old.)

Make no mistake: Gordie Howe was more than capable of achieving all three elements necessary to complete the celebrated triple play. He was a wizard at putting the biscuit in the basket, a magician at deftly slipping a pass through myriad sticks and skates and putting the disc on the tape of a teammate's stick, and he wasn't opposed to delivering a knuckle sandwich to a deserving adversary.

However, the tattered pages of the NHL record books show that he recorded only one Howe Hat Trick in his 32-year career in the NHL and the World Hockey Association. On December 22, 1955, in a game against the Boston Bruins, Howe (playing for the Detroit Red Wings) scored the tying goal, set up the winning 3–2 tally, and bested Beantown left winger Lionel Heinrich in a spirited tussle.

The Gordie Howe Hat Trick isn't an official statistic—in fact, the San Jose Sharks is the only franchise that lists the achievement in its media guide—but it is a widely acknowledged measurement of a skater's ability to play the game with both physical skill and artistic grace. The New York Rangers' Brendan Shanahan is the NHL's all-time leader in "Howe Hats." According to *The Hockey News*, Shanny scored a goal, recorded an assist, and had a fight nine times in the same game.

Q What popular sporting events of the early 1900s lasted six days?

A What sport lasted a day longer than the ancient Olympics, broke the race barrier before baseball, and caused more injuries than modern football? Why, turn-of-the-century bicycle racing, of course.

In 1900, the most popular sport in North America was the grueling phenomenon known as the six-day bicycle race. Usually held on indoor velodromes with wooden tracks, these events would pit teams of two riders against each other for 144 hours where they would alternate accruing laps with competing in sprinting events. These six-day events were not a sport for the faint of heart. At a race, as many as 70,000 fans would thrill to the sight of these powerful riders sustaining serious, often fatal, injuries and pushing themselves to the limits of endurance.

Like modern stock car racing, six-day cycling events used pacing vehicles. Originally, these were bicycles powered by two to five riders. But in 1895, English races began using primitive motorcycles. These new pace vehicles allowed the cyclists to travel faster, owing to the aerodynamic draft produced by the machines. Crowds thrilled to the speed and noise of these mechanical monsters, which weighed about 300 pounds each. It took two men to operate the motorcycles, one to steer and one to control the engine. They were also quite dangerous: A tandem pacer forced off the track in Waltham, Massachusetts on May 30, 1900, killed both riders and injured several fans. The advent of motorcycles increased the popularity of the six-day races for a time, but it waned with the arrival of a new vehicle spectators preferred over bicycles: the automobile.

Here are some of the sport's major players during its height:

Reggie McNamara (1887–1970): Dubbed the "Iron Man" of cycling, Australian Reggie McNamara had a seemingly inhuman capacity for the punishment and exertion that defined the six-day events. On the fourth day of a competition in Melbourne, McNamara underwent an emergency trackside operation without anesthesia to remove a large abscess "from his side." Though he lost a considerable amount of blood, he rose from the dust and, ignoring the entreaties of his trainer and doctor, resumed the race. In fact, his injuries on the track put him in the hospital so often that he wound up marrying an American nurse after a 1913 competition in New

York. He achieved several world records and defeated the French champions so soundly that they refused to ride against him.

Bobby Walthour (1878–1949): During his career, bicycling champion Bobby Walthour of Atlanta, Georgia, suffered nearly fifty collarbone fractures and was twice assumed to be dead on the track—only to rise and continue riding. By the time he was age 18, he was the undisputed champion of the South; soon he held the title of international champion and kept it for several years. In addition to making himself and cycling familiar to people all over the world, Walthour brought a great deal of prominence to his native Atlanta. Invigorated by his accomplishments, Atlanta built the Coliseum, one of the world's preeminent velodromes at the time.

Marshall "Major" Taylor (1879–1932): African American cyclist Major Taylor, the son of an Indianapolis coach driver, proved that endurance bicycling was a sport in which individual talent could not be denied. In an era of overt racism and discrimination, he rose through the ranks to become one of the highest paid athletes of his time. After relocating to the somewhat more race-tolerant Worcester, Massachusetts, Taylor began to rack up a string of victories in the six-day and sprinting competitions. Dubbed the "Worcester Whirlwind," Taylor toured the world, defeated Europe's best riders, and set several world records during his professional career.

Q What's the fastest pitch in baseball history?

A The April 1, 1985, issue of *Sports Illustrated* magazine featured an article about an up-and-coming pitcher in the New York Mets' farm system named Sidd Finch. Despite an unusual biography (he was born in an orphanage in England, attended Harvard, and studied yoga in Tibet) and some quirks (he wore a single heavy hiking boot while pitching), one extraordinary fact about Finch stood out: He could throw a pitch 168 miles per hour. No one had ever unleashed a pitch anywhere close to that speed.

Some Mets fans were beside themselves in anticipation of the big-league arrival of this can't-miss phenom. Alas, Finch turned out to be a product of the imagination of noted writer George Plimpton. The date of the article's publication should have been a clue.

In truth, the most powerful pitchers in baseball can throw a ball somewhere around 100 miles per hour. For what it's worth, Guinness World Records lists Nolan Ryan's 100.9-mile-per-hour delivery on August 20, 1974, as the fastest pitch ever thrown.

These days, most major-league ballparks post pitch-speed readings on their scoreboards. Problem is, some of these readings are unreliable—teams like to boost the numbers a bit to excite fans. While plenty of pitches purportedly have been clocked at speeds greater than Ryan's—the fastest, thrown by the Detroit Tigers' Joel Zumaya in 2006, was recorded at 104.8 miles per hour—there is no set standard or official governance of pitch-speed records.

In the end, Sidd Finch may have as much right to the title as Nolan Ryan or Joel Zumaya.

Q Who was the worst team in major league baseball history?

A The 1962 New York Mets and their record of 40-120? Ha! The 42-112 Pittsburgh Pirates of 1952? Please. The 2003 Detroit Tigers, who went 43-119? C'mon.

No, the worst team in professional baseball history was the 1899 Cleveland Spiders. Most teams experience an off-season, but in 1899, the Cleveland Spiders couldn't have been more off their game. Their record of 20-134 gave them a scintillating .130 winning percentage. They were good (or bad) enough to finish a mere 84 games out of first place. Yet just four years prior the Spiders had been the best team in baseball. What happened?

The Cleveland Spiders, so called because of the skinny appearance of many of their players, began life in baseball's National League in 1889. In 1892, led by future pitching great Denton True "Cy" Young (who was bought by the team for $300 and a new suit), the Spiders finished second in the league. In 1895, the Spiders won the Temple Cup, the forerunner to the World Series.

However, despite the large crowds that would attend Sunday games, playing baseball on that day was still controversial. In 1897, the entire Spiders team was thrown into the pokey for playing baseball on the Sabbath. The following season, Cleveland was forced to shift most of their Sunday games to other cities.

Attendance suffered, and the team stumbled to a record of 81-68. One other factor contributed to the Spiders' demise: Syndicate baseball. This meant that it was acceptable for owners of one National League team to own stock in another. Inevitably, the team with the better attendance and players drew most of the owner's attention and finances, while the lesser team suffered.

Syndicate baseball arrived in Cleveland in early 1899, when owner Frank Robison bought the St. Louis Browns at a sheriff's auction. He decided that St. Louis was a better market than Cleveland, and so he shipped all of the best Spiders there and renamed the new group—in case anyone missed the point—the Perfectos. Meanwhile, the absent Spiders were replaced by, well, anybody.

Robison's brother Stanley was put in charge of Cleveland. Stanley started off on the wrong foot with Cleveland fans by stating that he intended to operate the Spiders "as a sideshow." Faced with that encouraging news, fewer than 500 fans turned out for Cleveland's Opening Day double-header. Not surprisingly, the Spiders lost both games. The rout had begun.

And what a rout it was! After the first 38 games, the Spiders had 30 losses. Deciding that third baseman/manager Lave Cross was the problem, Robison sent him to St. Louis (which actually was a reward). With virtually no one showing up for the games, Stanley locked the Cleveland ballpark and announced that the Spiders would play their remaining "home" games on the road.

The dismal team—now dubbed the "Wanderers," "Exiles," and "Forsakens"—won just 12 more games the entire season. At one point they lost 24 games straight, which is still a record. They were so bad that after the Spiders beat the Baltimore Orioles, the Orioles' pitcher was fined and suspended. In the midst of all this, Cleveland sportswriter Elmer Bates compiled a tongue-in-cheek list of reasons to follow the Spiders. Among them:

1. There is everything to hope for and nothing to fear.
2. Defeats do not disturb one's sleep.
3. There is no danger of any club passing you.
4. You are not [always] asked..."What was the score?" People take it for granted that you lost.

On the last day of the season, a 19-year-old cigar stand clerk pitched for the Spiders; the team lost 19-3. After the game, the Spiders presented the team travel secretary with a diamond locket because, as the dedication said, he "had the misfortune to watch us in all our games." The following year Cleveland was dropped from the National League.

Which baseball card is worth the most?

 Honus Wagner was either the most noble of all early 20th-century baseball players—a man who cringed at the very thought of his likeness being used to hawk a tobacco product—or a guy who was ticked that he wasn't getting a big enough share of the profits.

Regardless of the reason, the "Flying Dutchman" pitched a fit when the American Tobacco Company, a cigarette manufacturer, released its T206 series of tobacco cards in 1909. Approximately 50 cards picturing Wagner in uniform with the Pittsburgh Pirates are estimated to have made it to cigarette packs back in the day before being yanked. Only a tiny percentage of those 50 made it to the late 20th-century marketplace.

Flash-forward a hundred years, and that T206 card, the "Holy Grail" among baseball card collectors, is considered the most valuable card of all time. One such exemplar has been owned by hockey Hall of Famer Wayne Gretzky, who—along with a business partner—purchased the T206 card for $451,000 in 1991. Gretzky later sold it in 1995 for $500,000 to Wal-Mart, which used it as part of a store promotion. The winner—a Florida postal worker— was thrilled...until she had to sell it to cover the taxes on her good fortune.

And so Wagner's travels continued as the card was auctioned for $640,000 and again on the online auction site eBay for almost twice that: $1.27 million. Oh, but the news just keeps getting better, as an anonymous collector with gobs of money shelled out $2.35 million for this cardboard classic in 2007. Looking to make a quick buck, that same collector turned around and sold it six months later...for a record $2.8 million.

Somewhere, a 110-year-old man is kicking himself for sticking his Honus Wagner card in the spokes of his bicycle.

Q How much did a trip to the ballpark cost in 1920?

A You can thank 19th-century entrepreneur Harry M. Stevens for many of the staples found nationwide at ballparks today. In 1885, Ohio entrepreneur Harry M. Stevens invented scorecards as a way to keep track of the players and the action (and to sell some advertising space). He sold them at various ballparks for five cents each. By the turn of the century he was also selling ice cream and sodas to baseball fans.

When sales proved slow on cold, early-season days at New York's Polo Grounds, he sent out some of his salespeople to buy "dachshund" sausages and buns, then encouraged them to yell, "Get 'em while they're red hot!" Thus the term "hot dog" was popularized. Even today, when fans can find everything from nachos to sushi at the ballpark, people still line up for the staples that have been sold for more than a century, including bags of peanuts and soda that is drunk through a straw (both of which were also Stevens's ideas).

Prices for everything at the ballpark have increased by leaps and bounds through the years, but this has become especially true in the past two decades as the corporate culture has provided a base of customers willing to pay more for better seats and fancier eats.

Some selected ballpark prices from selected seasons (not adjusted for inflation):

	1920	1942	1962	1980	2006
Program/Scorecard	$.10	$.10	$.25	$.50	$4.00
Hot Dog	$.10	$.15	$.35	$1.00	$4.50
Soda	$.05	$.10	$.25	$.55	$4.75
Beer	Prohibition	$.25	$.45	$1.00	$6.50
Box Ticket	$1.00	$2.20	$3.50	$6.00	$41.00

Q What's the farthest anyone has hit a baseball?

A There isn't a reliable answer, and here's why: While everything within the confines of the field of play in professional baseball—including the dimensions of those confines—is scrupulously measured and recorded, the stuff outside the field of play is up for grabs.

There are numerous falsehoods regarding the farthest anyone has hit a baseball. For years, *Guinness World Records* has stated that Mickey Mantle of the New York Yankees hit a ball 565 feet at Griffith Stadium in Washington, D.C., on April 17, 1953, calling it "the longest measured home run." Well, it turns out that it was measured to the point where a neighborhood kid picked up the ball, not necessarily where it actually landed.

Other similarly gargantuan blows have come into question. Dave Nicholson of the Chicago White Sox hit one at Chicago's Comiskey Park on May 6, 1964, that team "mathematicians" pegged at 573 feet. But as historian William J. Jenkinson pointed out, the mathematicians based their calculation on the belief that the ball cleared the roof; in fact, it hit the back of the roof before escaping the stadium.

The New York Times reported that a blast by Dave Kingman of the New York Mets at Chicago's Wrigley Field on April 14, 1976, went 630 feet. The homer, which bounced off a building across the street, was later measured at 530 feet, though even that number is based on conjecture.

By now, you've probably noticed that there hasn't been much hard science applied to determining the longest ball ever hit; instead, it's been a mishmash of speculation. However, that is changing. Greg Rybarcyzk, creator of the Web site Hit Tracker, measures the distance of every home run hit by using a complex formula that includes time of flight, initial trajectory, atmospheric conditions, and so on. If his calculations are wrong, it's going to take a wise man with a lot of time on his hands to prove them so.

Since Rybarcyzk's Hit Tracker began measuring homers in 2005, no one has hit a ball more than five hundred feet—the 490s is about as Herculean as a blast has gotten.

This somewhat supports the work of Robert Adair, a Yale physics professor who states in his book *The Physics of Baseball* that the farthest a human can possibly hit a baseball is 545 feet. Adair's claim calls into further dispute the dozens of anecdotal moon shots that are part of baseball lore, including Mantle's and Nicholson's. And while Adair's number doesn't answer the question, it at least puts us in the ballpark.

Q When was throwing a spitball outlawed in baseball?

A The spitball has had dozens of names, from "country sinker" to the "aqueous toss" and "humidity dispenser" or, more directly, "the wet one." But the spitball belongs in a larger class of pitches in which the ball is altered in one way or another to break or twist when it heads toward the batter. These pitches haven't always been fair, but they've usually done the trick.

Pitchers began seeking an advantage over hitters almost as soon as Jim Creighton developed the wrist snap in the 1850s. The rules were much simpler then, leaving more room for creative interpretation. So in 1868, when 16-year-old Bobby Matthews of the Lord Baltimores spat on the ball and fired it with the underhand stiff wrist the rules then required, the ball danced, and the batters went crazy.

In the 1890s, Clark Griffith, who amassed more than 200 wins in his pitching career, would bang the ball against his spikes, cutting it and leaving it subject to off-balance aerodynamic forces—thereby baffling hitters. In later years, pitchers would alter their gloves to leave a hole through which they could scrape the ball on a doctored ring. Or they would have a friendly teammate wear a belt with a sharp buckle and tear it against the ball as they warmed up before an inning.

In the early 1900s, Ed Walsh of the Chicago White Sox learned how to moisten a ball just right on the tips of his fingers so it would slide off and be harder to hit. Before long, the spitter was the pitch of choice for dozens of hurlers. Historians John Thorn and John Holway have said, "The dead-ball era could be called the doctored ball era."

Walsh's spitball was especially devastating because he could make it break four different ways: down and in, straight down, down and out, and up (which he threw underhand). So that the batters wouldn't know what to expect, Walsh put his hand to his face on every pitch, but he threw the spitter only about half the time. He and fellow spitball artist Jack Chesbro became the only two pitchers to win 40 games in one season in the 20th century.

After years of wild pitches (culminating in the death of Ray Chapman, who was hit in the temple by a pitched ball), baseball decided to clean up its act. Since the 1890s, it had been "illegal" for pitchers to damage a ball to alter pitches, but that rule was rarely enforced. The spitter was officially banned before the 1920 season (with stricter punishments for rule-breakers), although 17 pitchers were grandfathered in and allowed to throw it until their careers ended. The new rule outlawed spit, sandpaper, resin, talcum powder, and other "foreign substances" that produced trick pitches. So hurlers had to find better ways to cheat.

Some did and later admitted it; some have denied all wrongdoing. Hall of Famer Whitey Ford of the Yankees has been accused of using every creative trick he could muster, from gouging the ball with a ring, to covering one side of the ball with mud, to creating a special invisible gunk that he slathered on his fingers between innings.

Lew Burdette of the Braves in the 1950s always said that having the hitters think he had a spitter was just as good as actually throwing one. He'd wipe his hands on his pants and in his hair and then spit between his teeth.

But the all-time artist of loading the ball was Gaylord Perry, who used his wiles (and a lot of Vaseline) to win Cy Young Awards in both leagues. Perry's gyrations between each pitch were phenomenal. He'd grab here, scratch there, flick here, wipe there.

No one could possibly know what was coming. In all his years of cheating, Perry was caught just once.

Q What baseball team did the Royal Rooters root for?

A Sometimes the action on the field is less interesting than the action happening in the stands. Sometimes, loyal fans cheer their teams on to victory. And sometimes, when fans are at their most fanatic, they end up getting in the way of the game on the field.

One set of famous fans was the Royal Rooters, who cheered on the Boston Red Sox. The group was led by politico "Honey Fitz" Fitzgerald (President Kennedy's grandfather) and saloon owner "Nuf Ced" (because he always had the last word) McGreevey. They had a theme song, "Tessie," which they used to regale their team and distract the opposing team. In the first World Series game in 1903, the Royal Rooters even travelled to Pittsburgh and cheered on their team to victory.

The Royal Rooters marched together, traveled together, and taunted the opposition together. And they always—always—sat together, in the same block of seats at Fenway Park.

Well. Almost always. And when they were denied that tradition, the Rooters moved from the sidelines to the field.

The incident occurred on October 15, 1912, during Game 7 of the World Series. With the Red Sox up three games to two (Game 2 had ended in a tie), a Boston ticket clerk mistakenly sold the seats that belonged to the Royal Rooters. When the group arrived at the ballpark and found that they had no seats, they didn't handle it well. Just as the game was about to start, they broke through an outfield fence, disrupting fans and players, then marched around the field in a riotous scene.

By the time the police restored order and the game was able to begin, the Boston pitcher's arm had cooled off. He allowed five first-inning runs, a deficit the Sox were unable to make up. So the Rooters had effectively forced another Series game—something they had not intended, seats or no seats. The Rooters were so miffed that they refused to go to Game 8, although they were right there celebrating with everyone when Boston won the championship.

Though the original Royal Rooters are long gone, their spirit lives on; a version of "Tessie" turned up again as the official song of the Boston Red Sox during their 2004 World Series run.

Chapter 11

REMARKABLE PEOPLE

Q Who was the first African American player in the American League?

A Jackie Robinson's story has been well documented and celebrated. Larry Doby's story is not as well known, but that doesn't make it any less remarkable or his actions less courageous.

On April 15, 1947, Jackie Robinson trotted out onto Ebbets Field for the National League's Brooklyn Dodgers, smashing the color barrier that barred African Americans from major-league baseball.

On July 5, 1947, Larry Doby walked from the dugout of Comiskey Stadium in Chicago to pinch-hit for the Cleveland Indians, blazing the trail for African Americans in the American League.

Because Doby followed Robinson, some have deemed Doby's achievement less significant, and his story less compelling. "Jackie's number is hung in every ballpark in the country," former Cleveland player Ellis Burks said in 2003, in reference to Major League Baseball retiring Robinson's number 42. "But Larry Doby never did get enough recognition for what he did."

That shouldn't be the case, because Doby's accomplishment was every bit as important as Robinson's—and certainly as arduous. "It was eleven weeks between the time Jackie Robinson and I came into the majors," Doby said about the experience. "Eleven weeks. Whatever happened to him happened to me."

Whereas several Brooklyn Dodger players circulated a petition during spring training in 1947 refusing to play on the same field as Robinson, some of Doby's Cleveland teammates refused to shake his hand when he was first introduced in the Indian clubhouse, a moment he would recall as one of the most embarrassing of his life.

In his first game with the Indians, initially, none of the players volunteered to do warm-up tosses with him until player Joe Gordon stepped up. "You don't know what a terrible feeling that was," Doby later said. Like Robinson, Doby heard the racial slurs and verbal attacks from the fans and other players. Like Robinson, he was not allowed to stay in the same hotels or eat in the same restaurants as the rest of his teammates. Like Robinson, he had to brave his ordeal alone, having no black peer to take solace with on the field, in the dugout, or on the road.

But, also like Robinson, Doby persevered by maintaining a stoic dignity and excelling on the diamond. "I couldn't react to [prejudice] from a physical standpoint," he once explained. "My reaction was to hit the ball as far as I could." And hit it he did: He was a seven-time All-Star and won the American League home run crown in 1952 and 1954. He cemented his place in Cleveland sports history by helping lead the Indians to their last World Series title (so far) in 1948, batting .318 in the six-game series and belting the game-winning homer in Game 4. He was ranked with Joe DiMaggio and Duke Snider as one of the best center fielders of his era.

Some have suggested that it was actually Doby, not Robinson, who had the tougher go of things. Dodgers president Branch Rickey brought Robinson along slowly, allowing him to play 18 months in the minors before debuting in Brooklyn. Rickey protected Robinson, carefully planning and guiding the whole process so that Robinson could survive it. Robinson had the time to prepare himself for what lay ahead.

Contrast that to Doby, who made his major league debut one day after being signed from the Negro League Newark Eagles by Indians owner Bill Veeck. Doby's protection: two black Chicago police detectives who sat on the bench with him during only his first game to shield him from abusive fans.

Doby, however, never saw it that way. As he said later, "I look at myself as more fortunate than Jack. If I'd gone through hell in the minors, then I'd have to go through it again in the majors. Once was enough."

Larry Doby reached another landmark in 1962, when he became the second African American to sign with Japan's Nippon Professional Baseball League.

 Who is the only person to be inducted into both the Pro Football Hall of Fame and the Baseball Hall of Fame?

You might have caught this back on page 209, when we discussed the first group of men inducted in the Pro Football Hall of Fame. One of them was Robert "Cal" Hubbard, and thus far, he's the only man enshrined in both the Pro Football Hall of Fame and Baseball Hall of Fame.

Cal Hubbard was a legendary Packers offensive lineman of the 1920s and '30s—big and fast, he won four NFL championships, the first with the New York Giants and three others with the Green Bay Packers. But Hubbard didn't stop there. He began to spend his off-seasons as a baseball umpire, officiating in the minor leagues. He reached the majors as an American League umpire in 1936, his final year as a football player, and dispensed baseball justice for the next 15 years, working four World Series and three All-Star Games. His experience running football plays helped him design various patterns of positioning for umpires that are still used today. In later years, after an accident damaged his eyesight, he acted as a league supervisor.

Hubbard was inducted in the Pro Football Hall of Fame in 1963. He was inducted in the Baseball Hall of fame in 1976, a year before he died at the age of 76.

Robert "Cal" Hubbard has also been honored with induction to the Missouri Sports Hall of Fame, the College Football Hall of Fame, the Louisiana Sports Hall of Fame, and the Green Bay Packers Hall of Fame.

Q Which great female athlete once struck out Joe DiMaggio?

A It was the most unusual of baseball showdowns. Two of the 20th century's greatest sports icons stared each other down across a distance of 60 feet, 6 inches. At the plate: Joe DiMaggio, the Yankee legend whose Hall of Fame plaque would one day show three American League MVP Awards, two batting titles, and a record 56-game hitting streak. On the mound: a woman.

But this was no ordinary woman. She was, perhaps, the greatest female athlete of all time. Babe Didrikson Zaharias had been throwing harder, running faster, and playing better than the boys since she was a girl in Port Arthur, Texas. On this day, she was pitching for the barnstorming House of David men's team, a club whose players wore long beards. Zaharias's arm had impressed the team enough that her lack of a beard was easily overlooked.

The details of this legendary face-off between DiMaggio and Zaharias have become cloudy with the passage of time. However, DiMaggio once described it to writer Bert Sugar. "Struck him out on three pitches," Sugar said. The clincher was an overhand fastball.

Born Mildred Ella Didrikson, Babe earned her nickname after a Ruthian feat: smashing five home runs during a game in her youth. A natural at every pursuit she attempted, Didrikson excelled at basketball, diving, swimming, tennis, bowling, and lacrosse as a youngster. As talented as she was at this wide array of athletic aspirations, she made her first headlines and acquired her moniker playing the male-dominated sport of baseball. She could throw a baseball with alarming accuracy from astonishing distances, snare hotshot ground balls, and snag line drives with dexterity and grace.

It was her ability with the bat, however, that opened eyes and slackened jaws. She was so adept at hammering the horsehide that she drew instant comparisons to George Herman Ruth, the New York Yankees' Sultan of Swat who was known worldwide as the Babe. Didrikson's success with the stick earned her the same nickname, and she adopted the appellation with pride.

But as adept as she was on the diamond, Babe was also a standout on the basketball court at Beaumont High School. The Employers

Casualty Insurance Company of Dallas noticed her star status and enlisted her to play for the company's industrial league team, the Golden Cyclones. Between 1930 and 1932, she guided the team to the Amateur Athletic Union (AAU) national championship and was voted All-American each season. Her exceptional athletic versatility prompted the company to expand its women's sports program into track and field. The company sponsored Babe's involvement in the 1932 AAU championships, which served as an Olympic-qualifying tournament for the upcoming games. Babe competed in eight of ten events, winning five gold medals while setting world records in the javelin, 80-meter hurdles, high jump, and baseball throw.

That performance earned her a berth on the U.S. Olympic team, and she represented her country with distinction at the 1932 Summer Games in Los Angeles. Though she was technically a novice—she had never even seen a track and field meet until 1930—her competitive desire and prodigious prowess allowed her to overcome her inexperience with astounding results. Didrikson won Olympic gold in both the javelin and the 80-meter hurdles, breaking her own world records in the process. She also set a world record in the high jump, but her effort was downgraded from gold to silver-medal status because of a technicality: She cleared the record height by diving headfirst over the bar—a method so revolutionary that Olympic officials refused to award her a gold medal.

Following her unprecedented Olympic success, Didrikson didn't exactly settle into civilian life. She continued to barnstorm around the country, speaking on the rubber chicken circuit, appearing as a vaudeville novelty act playing harmonica while running on a treadmill, and playing basketball and baseball. In 1934, she spent the summer with the esteemed House of David baseball team, an amateur group with tremendous ability that toured the country playing—and often defeating—some of the best professional teams in the land. In that year, Zaharias pitched in two major-league spring training games in Florida. She threw the first inning of a Philadelphia Athletics match against Brooklyn, walking one batter but not allowing a hit. Two days later, she pitched an inning for the Cardinals against the Red Sox, yielding her first runs. She did not bat in either game, but in warm-ups she reportedly chucked a baseball from center field to home plate—a distance of 313 feet.

She also pursued a new passion, the game of golf. After only a few months of practice, Babe deemed herself competent for competitive play and won the second tournament she entered—the Texas Women's Amateur Championship in April 1935.

Didrikson went on to record 82 career amateur and professional victories—including 10 major titles. She captured a trio of U.S. Open crowns in 1948, 1950, and 1954 and strung together a remarkable and unprecedented 17 consecutive wins from April 1946 to August 1947, a feat no other duffer of either gender has been able to equal.

Didrikson was a founding member of the Ladies Professional Golf Association (LPGA) and continued to win tournaments with uncanny ease until 1954, when she was diagnosed with colon cancer. Fourteen weeks later, she returned to the links and won the U.S. Women's Open. Though noticeably slowed by her illness, she captured another pair of titles before succumbing to the disease in September 1956.

 Which ballplayer acquired the nickname "the splendid splinter"?

 Throughout baseball history, nicknames have been the name of the game. Colorful or descriptive, humorous or just plain fitting, creative monikers have added flavor to the game. In the 1930s, for example, the baseball-playing Dean brothers were called "Dizzy" and "Daffy."

Today, baseball nicknames are more often than not the effortless shortening of a name: A-Rod (Alex Rodriguez), Jetes (Derek Jeter), Junior (Ken Griffey, Jr.)...These nicknames could apply to anyone, anywhere. But back in the day, a ballplayer's nickname told you something about him and—occasionally—how he played the game. So we can refer to Babe Ruth as "The Sultan of Swat," dub Bob Ferguson "Death to Flying Things," and call Ted Willams "The Splendid Splinter."

Early in Williams's career, the Boston press dubbed him "The Splendid Splinter." The nickname made sense, given his spindly frame as a younger player. At 6'3", he weighed only 168 pounds, yet he could still crank out the hits.

Williams actually preferred two other nicknames: "The Kid," which is how he began referring to himself early in his Red Sox career, and "Teddy Ballgame," which was started rather inadvertently by the young son of a Boston photographer. When asked to name the ballplayer he most wanted to meet, the boy responded by saying, "Teddy...Teddy Ballgame." But sometimes, even when you don't choose it, a nickname sticks.

Q **Which new quarterback helped his team earn the nickname "The Greatest Show on Turf"?**

A Most of the gridiron gladiators who grasped glory in the Super Bowl brought a storied and successful pedigree into the decisive game, with numerous accolades and accomplishments on their resume before they stepped into the spotlight and basked in the limelight. Most, but not all.

Before he marched the St. Louis Rams to victory in Super Bowl XXXIV, Kurt Warner was barely a name in his own household. A bench jockey throughout much of his collegiate career at Northern Iowa, Warner was signed by the Green Bay Packers in 1994 but was unceremoniously handed his pink slip before the season even began. Out of prospects and cash, he took a job at a local grocery store in Cedar Falls, Iowa, for $5.15 an hour.

Undaunted by his early failures, Warner began to slowly climb the football ladder. He rode the buses in the Arena Football League and played before an average of 15,000 fans with the Amsterdam Admirals of NFL Europe, helping ensure that the experiment to introduce American football to European soccer fans was a laughable failure. Returning to the United States, Warner landed a job as the backup quarterback of the St. Louis Rams in 1998, which meant he stood on the sideline and held a clipboard on game days and took most of the hits during practices.

An injury to incumbent starter Trent Green early in the 1999 campaign put the ball in Warner's hands, and he ran, threw, and excelled with it. *Sports Illustrated* immediately recognized that he was unrecognizable and put him on the cover of their October 18 edition with the caption, "Who Is this Guy?" With Warner calling the signals, the Rams became known as "The Greatest Show on Turf" and rode Warner's arm and calm grace under pressure all the way to the Super Bowl, where they dispatched the Tennessee Titans by a 23–16 score. Warner set a litany of Super Bowl records, including most passing yards and most pass attempts without an interception, and was named the game's MVP.

Q Who was the first and only heavyweight champion to retire undefeated?

A Born on September 1, 1923, in Brockton, Massachusetts, Rocco Francis Marchegiano was the heavyweight champion of the world from 1952 to 1956. To this day, with 43 knockouts to his credit, he remains the only heavyweight champion in boxing history to retire without a defeat or a draw.

When he was a year old, Rocky Marciano survived a near-fatal bout of pneumonia. This was perhaps the first evidence of the strength and resilience that led him to spend his childhood and young adulthood wrestling and playing baseball and football. He worked out on homemade weight-lifting equipment, including a makeshift heavy bag formed from an old mailbag that hung from a tree in his backyard. He dropped out of high school in tenth grade and worked as a ditchdigger, sold shoes, and found employment at a coal company.

In 1943, Marciano was drafted into the army, where he spent two years ferrying supplies across the English Channel to Normandy. During his stint in the military, Marciano won the 1946 amateur armed forces boxing tournament. He ended his amateur year with an 11–3 record—the last time Marciano ever experienced a loss.

In 1947, Marciano tried out for the Chicago Cubs baseball team but was cut three weeks later. Subsequently, he turned professional in the boxing ring. *Sports Illustrated* reported, "He was too short, too light, and had no reach....Rough and tough, but no finesse."

Marciano's hometown fans were believers, and they traveled in groups to watch his fights. When Rocky had an opponent ready to go down, they would yell, "Timmmberrr!" as they would for a falling tree, and the audience would go wild.

Rocky catapulted to stardom in 1951, when he was pitted against Joe Louis, his most formidable opponent and also his childhood idol. The match, which was the last of Louis's career, was aired on national television. Marciano KO'd Louis in the eighth round—and later sobbed in Louis's dressing room after the fight.

Marciano's trainer, Charley Goldman, taught Rocky his trademark technique—a short, overhand right to the jaw. This move served Marciano well when, in the 13th round against the defending heavyweight champion, lagging behind in points and struggling offensively, he suddenly KO'd Jersey Joe Walcott. The year was 1952.

Firmly established as a "marquee" fighter, Marciano went on to defend his title six times, including a first-round knockout victory in a 1953 rematch with Walcott and another knockout win over Roland La Starza later that year. With a left and a quick right to the jaw, Marciano won a decision against Ezzard Charles in 1954. But fans had a moment of panic when, in a rematch later that year, Marciano nearly lost his title in the sixth round. Charles cut Marciano's nose so badly that his corner trainer couldn't stop the bleeding. When the ring doctor considered stopping the fight, Marciano erupted against Charles and knocked him out in the eighth round. Ding! Victory was Marciano's.

A year later, despite organized crime enticements to throw the fight, Rocky KO'd European champion Don Cockell in an exciting nine rounds. Marciano's last fight was in Yankee Stadium on September 21, 1955. He knocked out Archie Moore in the ninth round as more than 400,000 people watched over closed-circuit television.

Marciano spent his retirement years working as a boxing show host and commentator and making personal appearances. He died at the age of 46 when a small private plane he was riding in crashed into a tree as it attempted to land in Newton, Iowa.

Inducted into the Boxing Hall of Fame in 1990, Rocky Marciano was honored in 1999 on a commemorative U.S. postage stamp. Marciano lives on through a myriad of books, films, and of course, in the minds and hearts of fans.

And although he may not rank among the top five boxers of all time, one sportswriter summed Marciano up accurately: "If all the heavyweight champions of all time were locked together in a room, Marciano would be the only one to walk out."

Q What sport can claim the "Fabulous Moolah"?

 In the mid-1950s, women's roles were as clearly defined as they were limited. For many women in the United States, the burgeoning "baby-boom" spelled out their fate: They would become housewives. It was also an era of high femininity and manners, where popular culture dictated what was deemed "ladylike" or not.

Still, amid this model, fringe elements were flowering. In professional wrestling, a new women's division took these accepted roles of femininity and stood them flat on their cauliflower ears. Under this entertaining banner, tough, self-assured women were suddenly tossed into the white-hot spotlight. Literally. Among the standout acts was a woman named Moolah.

Lillian Ellison hit the wrestling game at the perfect time. Women were screaming for excitement, and men were eager for the next gimmick. But timing wasn't something that Ellison was overly concerned with. She moved to her own beat and set her own goals. In the early 1950s, she married and became a very young mother as a teenager. The union would last only two years, but it reinforced Ellison's free-spirit outlook on life. Despite having a baby to raise, Ellison, an ardent wrestling fan, decided to suit up and give the professional ranks a shot. History was about to be made.

As the "Fabulous Moolah" Ellison gave both genders what they wanted. With her signature moves, such as the "Big Punch," the "School Girl Roll Up," and the "Spiral Backbreaker," Moolah was unlike anything wrestling fans had ever seen. In 1956, she would become the World Wide Wrestling Federation Women's Champion. It's a title she would hold until 1984. She recaptured it again in 1985, 1986, and 1999. She went on to wrestle in Japan, Mexico, Canada, and throughout Europe.

While Moolah was adept at delivering pile-drivers and subjecting opponents to painful half-nelsons, her appearance was one of pure utility. With her tough-as-nails grimace and strong, stocky shape, Moolah was as hard as she looked, and she didn't mind playing the villain. "I loved when they got mad at me," she said. "They called me all kinds of names. I said: 'Call me anything you want. You don't write my check.'"

Over the years, women's roles in wrestling have had other facets. Some women weren't wrestlers at all, but the supposed girlfriends of wrestlers, each handpicked for their attributes. Perhaps the most famous of the girlfriend archetype was Miss Elizabeth, the gorgeous companion/manager of wrestler "Macho Man" Randy Savage during the late 1980s and early '90s. Often rival wrestlers, such as George "The Animal" Steele and Hulk Hogan, would develop crushes on Elizabeth, but she fawned over her belligerent man, snaring the hearts of wrestling fans everywhere. Wrestling honchos seized on this sexpot phenomenon and filed it for future reference: They would eventually create a composite wrestling figure that included the athleticism of Fabulous Moolah coupled with the sex appeal of Miss Elizabeth.

While part of the sport's draw had always included the allure of attractive women in skimpy clothing, today's women in professional wrestling are more va-va-voom than ever. Nowadays, a wrestler like the tan, blonde Michelle McCool is as much a pinup diva as she is an athlete. Some might argue that women's wrestling has taken a step back from Moolah's day. With ultra-sexy stars like Velvet Sky, So-Cal Val, and Angelina Love, it appears the women's cheesecake factor matters at least as much as their devastating drop-kicks and sinister suplexes. On the other hand, the popularity of female wrestling has reached new heights. Perhaps it's time to classify this new breed as what they really are: sexy and capable. It's safe to assume that the Fabulous Moolah would have no problem with such a tantalizing union.

Q How many records did Babe Ruth hold at the time of his death?

A No one in baseball history has matched the achievements of the most well-rounded player of all time: George Herman "Babe" Ruth, pitcher and slugger extraordinaire.

A kid of the streets who learned to play ball while he was an "inmate" at St. Mary's Industrial School for Boys, 19-year-old George made the majors with the Boston Red Sox in 1914. Starting the next year, he went 78–40 with an ERA under 2.30 in helping the club to three World Series titles over four seasons. The left-hander completed a Series-record 29 consecutive scoreless innings in 1918, yet he was such a successful hitter that manager Ed Barrow began giving him outfield assignments on non-pitching days. The 6'2" giant liked the arrangement, and when he was allowed to roam the outfield almost exclusively in 1919, he hit an ML-record 29 home runs.

Theatrical producer and Red Sox owner Harry Frazee was not impressed. Needing money for his latest show and believing the uninhibited Ruth and his exorbitant $10,000 salary were to blame for a sixth-place slide in 1919, Frazee sold Babe to the New York Yankees in January 1920 for $125,000—plus a $300,000 loan on Fenway Park. Babe put his stamp of approval on the stupidest move in baseball history with a record-shattering 54 homers that year—more homers than 14 of 16 major-league teams compiled—and the spark was lit. Fans wanted excitement after the hard realities of World War I and the Black Sox scandal, and Ruth supplied it, showing that one swing could accomplish what had previously taken a series of bunts, steals, and slides.

He was the quintessential hero of the Roaring '20s, a ham for the cameras who enjoyed having every move followed and could back up his bravado. Dominating as no player before or since, he averaged 47 home runs and 133 RBI during the decade when just four other players hit as many as 40 homers even once. Over his career, Ruth would lead the Yankees to seven pennants and four World Series championships (hitting fifteen homers in Series play), despite regular indulgences in women, booze, and food. He drew suspensions from his managers and screams of delight from kids—and it was the kids who seemed to matter to him most.

Even when his 94–46 pitching mark is not factored in, Ruth's records are remarkable. He slugged .849 in a single season (1920) and averaged a .690 slugging and .474 on-base percentage over his career. When the .342 lifetime hitter retired, his 714 home runs were about twice as many as his nearest competitor. That career total and Babe's season high of 60 homers in 1927 have both since been topped, but his impact on the game remains undisputed. He was baseball's most beloved performer—and its finest.

When Babe Ruth died, he owned 56 major-league records plus ten more AL marks—including the best winning percentage for a pitcher, lifetime, against the New York Yankees.

Q Who was Simonya Popova?

 A September 2002 issue of *Sports Illustrated* told the world of an unstoppable 17-year-old tennis force named Simonya Popova, a Russian from Uzbekistan and a media dream who seemed too good to be true: 6'1", brilliant at the game, fluent in English, candid, busty, and blonde. She came from an appealing late-Soviet proletarian background and had a father who was often quoted in Russian-nuanced English. But she wouldn't be competing in the U.S. Open—her father forbade it until she turned 18.

The magazine verged on rhapsody as it compared Popova to Ashley Harkleroad, Daniela Hantuchová, Elena Dementieva, and Jelena Dokic. Editors claimed that, unlike Popova, all of these women were public-relations disappointments to both the Women's Tennis Association (WTA) and sports marketing because they chose to resist media intrusions to concentrate on playing good tennis. As a result, U.S. tennis boiled down to Venus and Serena Williams, trailed by a

pack of hopefuls and won't-quite-get-theres. The gushing article concluded with this line: "If only she existed."

Popova was too good to be true. The biography was fiction, and her confident gaze simply showcased someone's digital artistry.

Some people got it. Many didn't, including the media. They bombarded the WTA with calls: Who was Popova and why wasn't she in the Open? The article emphasized what many thought—the WTA was desperate for the next young tennis beauty. WTA spokesperson Chris DeMaria called the story "misleading and irritating" and "disrespectful to the great players we have." Complaining that some people didn't read to the end of articles, he said, "We're a hot sport right now and we've never had to rely on good looks."

Sports Illustrated claimed it was all in grand fun. It hardly needed to add that it was indulging in puckish social commentary on the sexualization of women's tennis.

What did manager Casey Stengel call rookies?

A Casey Stengel spent 55 years as a player and manager with a style, a sense of humor, and a language uniquely his own. As he might have put it: "There comes a time in everyone's life, and I've had plenty of them."

Charles Dillon Stengel was born in Kansas City in 1890 and made his major-league debut with the Brooklyn Dodgers in 1912. A fair hitter and outfielder, Stengel played fourteen seasons, mostly with the Dodgers and New York Giants, where he worked under legendary managers Wilbert Robinson and John McGraw. He gained a reputation as a clown, which was cemented in 1918 when, as a member of the Pittsburgh Pirates, he gave booing fans at Ebbets Field the bird, literally—he removed his cap and out flew a sparrow. "The higher-ups complained that I wasn't showing a serious attitude by hiding a sparrow in my cap," he later said, "but I said any day I get three hits, I am showing a more serious attitude than a lot of players with no sparrows in their hats."

"The Ol' Perfessor" piloted some of the best and worst teams of his time, amassing a 1,905–1,842 record over twenty-five seasons. After managing the talent-poor Dodgers (1934–36) and Boston Braves (1938–43), his break came when he was unexpectedly named manager of the New York Yankees in 1949. His appointment was unpopular with fans and the press, who couldn't believe the stodgy franchise would hire such a joker, but Casey had the last laugh: His Yankees would win ten pennants and seven World Series titles over the next twelve years.

As a manager, Stengel proved to have a keen eye for talent, often using positional platoons and his bullpen brilliantly. ("The secret of managing is to keep the guys who hate you away from the guys who are undecided," he said.) His skill with language—stream-of-consciousness ramblings peppered with large amounts of humor and nuggets of truth and practicality—was known as "Stengelese." He called rookies "green peas." A good fielder was a "plumber," and a tough ballplayer was someone who could "squeeze your earbrows off." Another example of classic Stengelese came when he said: "I don't know if he throws a spitball, but he sure spits on the ball."

Stengel was a master of the malaprop and the mixed metaphor, and with his humor and ability to turn a phrase he engaged writers, deflected attention from his players, and sparked interest in his clubs. These were key advantages throughout his career, especially when managing the dismal expansion New York Mets, whom he led from their founding in 1962 until a hip injury midway through the 1965 season ended his professional career at age 75. He was inducted into the Hall of Fame a year later.

Q Who was the oldest man to take the plate in a professional baseball game?

A When we think of baseball legends, we usually place them into one category: player, manager, or pioneer. But there are some icons who defy typecasting, and Buck O'Neil—one of baseball's greatest ambassadors—was one of them.

Buck O'Neil was a solid player in the Negro Leagues, with a career batting average of .288. The first baseman was a strong clutch hitter and had a league-leading .353 average in 1946; the next year he hit .358. He went on barnstorming tours with teammate Satchel Paige, played in the 1942 Black World Series, and was named to the East-West All-Star Game (the Negro Leagues' celebrated all-star game) in 1942, '43, and '49.

Yet there was so much more to Buck O'Neil than what he accomplished as a player. In 1948, he became manager of the Kansas City Monarchs. He won four Negro League pennants, led his clubs to two appearances in the Black World Series, and guided his teams to a perfect record of 4–0 in the East-West Game. The Negro Leagues began to dissolve in the 1950s, and O'Neil segued into a career with the major leagues. Joining the Chicago Cubs as a scout, O'Neil played crucial roles in signing Hall of Famers Lou Brock and Ernie Banks and quality major-leaguers like Joe Carter and Oscar Gamble. O'Neil also became the first African-American coach in major-league history, joining the Cubs' "College of Coaches" (which unsuccessfully employed a group of managers rather than just one) in the early 1960s.

O'Neil's contributions to baseball reached far off the field. After leaving scouting and coaching, O'Neil probably did more than anyone else to promote the legacy of the Negro Leagues. Whether charming audiences on Ken Burns' *Baseball* documentary or appearing on David Letterman's talk show, or through his work as a voting member of the Hall of Fame's Veterans Committee, O'Neil always did his best to praise the abilities and personalities of other Negro League stars. Ever modest about himself, he said that Oscar Charleston was the equal of Ty Cobb and praised Satchel Paige for bringing out the best in everyone—even the opposition.

O'Neil's storytelling greatly enhanced the public's knowledge and familiarity with the Negro Leagues, which had been largely overlooked until the 1990s. In 2000, O'Neil visited the Hall of Fame and discussed the ability that black players showed when they barnstormed against white teams featuring major-leaguers. "They [the major-leaguers] were just out there for a payday, but we wanted to prove a point that they weren't superior," O'Neil told the Cooperstown audience. "So we would stretch that single into a double, that double into a triple, that triple into a home run. This was Negro Leagues baseball, this was the baseball Jackie Robinson brought to the major leagues."

O'Neil emerged as an unofficial ambassador for the sport, exposing younger generations to the rich culture of the Negro Leagues.

Even in Buck's final summer, he persisted in advancing the awareness of black baseball. He continued his work as the chair of the Negro Leagues Museum, which he had started through tireless promotional and fundraising efforts. And in August, 2006, he achieved an unusual place in baseball history when he became the oldest man—at 94 years of age—to take the plate in a professional game.

O'Neil passed away on October 6, 2006, at the age of 94.

Who is nicknamed "The Old Arbitrator" on his Hall of Fame plaque?

 There have been other fine umpires—Al Barlick, Doug Harvey, Billy Evans. But there was only one Bill Klem.

Try to start a discussion that begins, "Who was the greatest [blank] of all time?" and you'll be in for some argument—unless the blank is "umpire." In that case, the answer is unquestionably Bill Klem. He was so good, and it was so obvious that he was so good, that for 16 of his record-setting 37-year National League career he only umpired behind the plate. That wasn't a reward for years of quality service—it started the first day he umped in the major leagues. He was uniquely skilled at calling balls and strikes.

Klem wasn't large, but he commanded respect because of his hard work and integrity. He took grief from some of the game's legendary grief-givers, but when the heat got to be too much, Klem would draw a line in the dirt with his toe, announce, "Don't cross the Rio

Grande," and turn his back. Anyone who crossed that line was headed for the showers. He was often called "The Old Arbitrator," and that nickname (which Klem loved) is on his Hall of Fame plaque. But if you called him "Catfish" (because of his looks), you were tossed immediately.

Klem pioneered the inside chest protector, which allowed for a better view of the pitch than the protectors that were previously worn outside the shirt. And he was one of the first to use hand signals for strikes and fouls. He umpired 104 World Series games in 18 Series—almost twice as many Series as any other ump—and he worked at the first All-Star Game in 1933. When he retired in 1941 at age 67, he was the oldest ump in baseball history.

Klem did one very important thing that many umpires never do, although they should: wait. He would hesitate and let the facts clarify themselves in his mind before making a call. Once when Klem paused before signaling safe or out, the frustrated catcher shouted, "Well, what is he?" Klem answered, "He ain't nothing till I call it."

Q What were some of Bill Veeck's wackiest stunts?

A One man seemed to have the magic touch when it came to boosting attendance at baseball games, and doing it fast. That man was Bill Veeck, and he kept fans in stitches with gimmicks and goofiness for years.

Bill Veeck was literally born into baseball. His father was president of the Chicago Cubs. The junior Veeck grew up in the ballpark, working as everything from a soda-pop vendor and ticket taker to groundskeeper (he claimed to have planted the ivy on the outfield walls of Wrigley Field) before moving up to club treasurer while he took night courses in business, accounting, and engineering.

In 1941, Veeck bought the American Association Milwaukee Brewers. He was just 27 years old, but he was already exploding with ideas. He never announced his promotions ahead of time, so folks would show up at the park with no idea what to expect. What they received were giveaways such as live lobsters, buckets of nails, or hosiery. They also got fireworks, live bands, and ballet. Anything could happen, and the fans loved it.

Veeck was unlike any other owner. While the other big-league moguls still wore steamed shirts and stickpins, Veeck never—ever—wore a tie. He much preferred the company of the bleacher fans to that of millionaires and movie stars. He spent his time during the games out in the stands, chatting with the fans, joining them for a beer, talking baseball. He asked the fans what they wanted, and he listened to their answers.

As owner of the Cleveland Indians, Veeck had his greatest success. He integrated the American League by signing Larry Doby in 1947. (Veeck allegedly received 20,000 pieces of hate mail about the signing and replied to each one by hand.) When he persuaded living legend Satchel Paige to join his team in '48, many called it a ridiculous publicity stunt. But it turned out to be anything but when Paige (at age 42, the oldest rookie in major-league history), went 6–1 in 72.2 innings, recorded an ERA of 2.48, and threw three complete games and two shutouts in his seven starts. The Indians won the pennant and the World Series in 1948, and fans came out in record numbers.

Veeck bought the St. Louis Browns in 1951, and that year he engineered a stunt designed to send the fans home chuckling and the baseball powers huffing and puffing in dismay. The fans were there to help celebrate the 50th anniversary of the American League; everyone received a slice of birthday cake as they entered the gate. Between games of the doubleheader, a fake birthday cake was rolled onto the field, and out of it jumped 3'7" Eddie Gaedel, wearing a Browns uniform with number 1/8 on the back. His job was to crouch down and ensure he'd get a walk. He did, and the fans went crazy.

Another memorable Veeck promotion was "Grandstand Managers' Day" on August 24, 1951, in which more than 1,000 St. Louis Browns fans decided on the game strategy while manager Zack Taylor sat alongside the dugout, propped up his feet, and drank an orange soda while he counted the fans' votes. The fans were given signs that said "YES" or "NO." Before the game, they held up these cards to select the Browns' starting lineup. During the game, they used these cards to vote on such questions as "Infield In?" or "Bunt?" The lineup choice was probably the fans' best decision. They replaced the regular starting catcher and first baseman with bench-sitters Sherm Lollar and Hank "Bow Wow" Arft. Each wound up with two RBI; Lollar had a homer and a double. The Browns, who had lost four of their previous five games, snapped the streak with a 5–3 crowd-managed win. Then they lost their next five.

In 1959, Veeck bought the Chicago White Sox and continued his fun-filled promotions. He created the exploding scoreboard that set off fireworks when a Sox player homered. And it was Veeck's idea to have Harry Caray lead the crowd in singing "Take Me Out to the Ball Game" during the seventh-inning stretch, a tradition that moved with Harry from Comiskey Park to Wrigley Field in 1982.

Any attempt to categorize Bill Veeck will inevitably result in slamming into a few walls of contradictions. Was he simply a ruthless (self) promoter who delighted in blowing the buttons off stuffed shirts? Was he truly the fans' owner, the man who cared for them more than anything? Was he merely a hustler, a Barnum, primarily a con man? Was he a savvy baseball intellect, or was he just lucky?

The answer to the final question is probably easiest. From 1947 through 1964, the New York Yankees were toppled from their habitual perch atop the American League just three times—twice by a team Veeck owned (1948 Indians, 1959 White Sox) and once by a team he had built (1954 Indians). If Veeck didn't always know how to make money running a team, he knew how to make money selling it. Every deal he made showed substantial profits. His teams set attendance records in Cleveland and Chicago, and he quintupled attendance in St. Louis.

Even when Bill Veeck made a mistake, he turned it into good publicity (or at least a good laugh). But perhaps the trait that most clearly defined the huge and paradoxical style of Bill Veeck was his sheer lust for life. Despite living in severe pain (he was said to have had 36 different operations), he never let it hold him back. After he died, one of his obituaries noted that if a life is measured not by how long it is, but by how full it is, "the old rapscallion [Veeck] must have turned over the odometer a few times."

Q How much could Joe Rollino lift?

 New York has had more than its fair share of colorful characters with unique stories, but few could outstrip the feats of The Great Joe Rollino. A Coney Island strongman who once purportedly lifted 475 pounds with his teeth and 635 pounds with one finger, he still took a daily five-mile stroll around his Brooklyn neighborhood—until a car struck him at age 104.

Standing just five foot five and weighing between 125 and 150 pounds, Mighty Joe was, relative to his size, one of the most powerful men alive, not just in terms of muscle strength but also with regard to individual body parts. Think about it: How come his weightlifting teeth weren't shattered or ripped from his gums, or the back with which he shifted 3,200 pounds didn't succumb to the slipped disc or lumbago that any normal person might suffer? No doubt about it, Joe was a tough guy, and he enjoyed demonstrating and talking about this virtually until he took his last breath.

Born on March 19, 1905, to Italian immigrants who presented him with thirteen siblings, Rollino spent even his earliest years building his body and flexing his muscles while training with America's first great strongman, Warren Lincoln Travis. After touring the United States as a boxer under the name of Kid Dundee, Rollino began showing off his strength as a Coney Island performer. Squashing nails with his gnashers and bending coins with his bare hands—you name it, The World's Strongest Man (as he liked to call himself) could do it. He labored as a longshoreman, served as a bodyguard to film star Greta Garbo, and got to know Harry Houdini. While in the Pacific during World War II, he earned a Silver Star, a Bronze Star, and three Purple Hearts (he took shrapnel in his legs and rescued several soldiers on the field of battle by grabbing and transporting each of them under one arm).

Aside from working out, part of Joe's secret was a healthy lifestyle that included yogurt and wheat germ long before they were popular. Joe abstained from meat, booze, and cigarettes. What's more, he took frequent swims in the Atlantic Ocean, regardless of whether it was lukewarm or freezing. As far as he was concerned, the colder, the better. During one winter in the 1950s, when the police didn't have the necessary protective gear to jump into icy waters, Joe retrieved the bodies of two people who had drowned in Prospect Park. A couple of decades later, in January 1974, a six-degree day saw the then 68-year-old "Puggy" (as his acquaintances called him) join a half dozen other members of the appropriately named Iceberg Athletic Club for a swim in the frigid waters off Coney Island. Nothing was too daunting for Mr. Rollino.

A longtime member of the not-for-profit, New York-based Association of Oldetime Barbell & Strongmen, which educates people about the hazards of drug use and the benefits of drug-free weightlifting and other sporting activities, Joe was handing out free advice to fellow "Iron Game" participants when celebrating his 103rd birthday at a Brooklyn restaurant. And he was still bending quarters with his teeth and regaling people with tales of his past achievements. "Fighters would hit me in the jaw and I'd just look at them," he told thesweetscience.com. "You couldn't knock me out." However, just before seven in the morning on January 11, 2010, "Old Man Joe" took one hit he couldn't shake off.

After buying newspapers at a local deli, 104-year-old Joe Rollino was struck by a Ford Windstar as he crossed Bay Ridge Parkway in Dyker Heights. He suffered a broken pelvis and severe head and chest injuries and died shortly after. His friend Charlie Laird told the *New York Daily News*, "Father Time didn't stand a chance against Joe Rollino. It took all the speed and might of a minivan, and I'm shocked that that was even able to take him down."

Q How many consecutive games did Cal Ripken play?

 The Setting: Oriole Park at Camden Yards; September 6, 1995

The Magic: Cal Ripken, Jr., breaking Lou Gehrig's "unbreakable" consecutive-game streak.

We don't just want our baseball heroes to be good; we want them to be good for a long time. Lou Gehrig's incredible record of 2,130 consecutive games had been a testament to his greatness. It seemed to be a feat that no one else could achieve...until Cal Ripken came along, playing inning after inning, game after game, year after year. Ripken's appearance in every game for more than thirteen seasons is especially monumental when you realize that during his streak more than 3,700 players spent time on the disabled list.

That September night in Baltimore, as Ripken prepared to beat Gehrig's streak, President Bill Clinton and Vice President Al Gore were in the stands, as were Joe DiMaggio and Frank Robinson. The crowd of more than 46,000 cheered for Cal when he took the field, when he batted in the second, and when he homered in the fourth. But when the last out was made in the top of the fifth with the Orioles leading (thus making it an official game), the ovation was deafening. Ripken left the dugout three times to acknowledge the cheers.

Finally his teammates Bobby Bonilla and Rafael Palmeiro convinced Cal to take a lap around the field. "If you don't, we'll never get this game going again," they said. Cal obligingly circled the field, waving to fans, shaking hands and slapping palms. The outpouring of affection lasted more than twenty minutes. But then it was time to get back to work, and the Orioles went on to beat the Angels 4–2.

And Ripken just kept going, playing another 501 games before ending his streak at 2,632 in 1998. In a game sometimes known for its overblown paychecks and egos, Ripken proved to be a class act year after year after year. As of this printing, his record still stands. In fact, Ripken and Gehrig remain the only people to break the barrier of 2,000 consecutive games played.

CHAPTER 12

THE ODD, THE OBSCURE, AND THE JUST PLAIN STRANGE

Q **What happens when animals get on the baseball field?**

A Rarely do animals and baseball go hand-in-hand, but some key moments on the field have made animals the stars of the show.

Ballplayers know to expect the unexpected, to try to be prepared for whatever pitches, hits, or plays they might encounter. But sometimes the unexpected arrives in a different package—a furry or feathered one—when an animal makes a surprise appearance on the field.

Even the best batters admit that hitting Randy Johnson's fastball isn't easy, but a dove flying a bit too close to the action at a 2001 spring-training game certainly made solid, if not tragic, contact. Johnson's seventh-inning delivery, intended for Giants outfielder Calvin Murray, hit the bird instead. Feathers erupted, and the ball—and what was left of the bird—ricocheted into foul territory behind the first base line. The delivery was ruled a non-pitch.

On August 4, 1983, Dave Winfield of the Yankees had a similar "fowl" incident, but with more dramatic consequences. Between innings of a game against the Blue Jays in Exhibition Stadium, Winfield struck and killed a seagull while throwing in the outfield. He was arrested after the game on a charge of cruelty to animals. He posted $500 bail and was scheduled for a court date the next time the Yankees visited Toronto, but the charges were later dropped. If convicted, Winfield could have faced up to six months in jail. "They say he hit the gull on purpose," remarked Yankees manager Billy Martin. "They wouldn't say that if they'd seen the throws he'd been making all year."

Occasionally in player-animal matchups, it's the players who fall victim. A stray black cat made an eerie appearance in a critical Mets–Cubs game on September 9, 1969. Just as Billy Williams dug into the batter's box in the first inning, the cat darted out from beneath the Shea Stadium stands, stopped briefly to consider Williams, slinked past Ron Santo in the on-deck circle, then headed for the visiting dugout, where Mets fans believe he hissed at manager Leo Durocher.

Was it an omen? It marked the last night of the season that the Cubs went to bed in first place. Despite holding a lead as large as ten games over the Mets on August 13, the Cubs' 7–1 loss the night the cat appeared reduced their lead to a half-game, which the surging Mets erased the next night. Like the cat, the Cubs weren't heard from again.

Dogs aren't always man's best friend. Marge Schott, the brash one-time owner of the Reds, was known for her inappropriate behavior and comments and also for her love of animals. Her beloved St. Bernards, Schottzie and Schottzie 02, like several of her struggling Reds teams, were known to leave a mess on the Riverfront Stadium field. However, it was the dogs, not the players, who graced the cover of the team's media guides.

In September 1998, Mark McGwire arrived in Cincinnati fresh from breaking Roger Maris's home run record, only to be humiliated when Schott forced him to pet Schottzie and rub the dog's hair on his Cardinals jersey for good luck. Unfortunately, McGwire was not so lucky. He's allergic to dogs.

In March 2005, a spring-training game between the Rockies and the Diamondbacks was called after a swarm of bees invaded the field. Darren Oliver, pitching for Colorado, was literally chased off the mound by the swarm. He suspected coconut-scented gel in his hair was to blame. However, after he fled, the bees chased shortstop Sergio Santos out to deep center field before umpires stepped in. "I guess we've got to call that a 'bee' game," said Arizona manager Bob Melvin.

Q Where do toe wrestlers complete?

A This little piggy went to the World Toe Wrestling Championship held annually in July in Derbyshire, England. The contestants sit facing each other at a "toedium"—which is, of course, a stadium for toes—and try to push each other's bare foot off a small stand that is called a "toesrack." Three-time champion Paul Beech calls himself the "Toeminator."

Toe wrestling began in the town of Wetton in the 1970s; to no one's surprise, it was invented at a pub. The international sport is governed by the World Toe Wrestling Organization, which once applied for Olympic status but was rejected.

 ## What sport does the Tournament de la Saint-Louis celebrate?

 Competitors in the Tournament de la Saint-Louis take to the water—not for swimming, diving, or boating, but for jousting.

Water (or sea) jousting captures all the action of medieval jousting without that sport's messy mauling and death. Nevertheless, it features fearsome competitors such as the "Unrootable" Casimir Castaldo and Vincent Cianni, "the man of 100 victories."

The drill is simple: Two boats are rowed toward each other. (Modern times have invaded the sport—some contests allow boats with motors.) When helm nears helm, competitors perched on protruding platforms draw their lances, hold up their shields, and get busy. Last one standing gets the girl, or at least a moment of glory. And the vanquished? That wet critter gets to joust another day.

The sport dates back to 2780 B.C., when Egyptian bas-reliefs depicted nautical jousts that were possibly a genuine form of warfare. The ancient Greeks and Romans carried on the tradition. Although the sport lapsed in popularity, it began to come back into its own in the 1400s and 1500s.

Today, the most prestigious event is the Tournament de la Saint-Louis held in Sète, France, every August. Since 1743 it has attracted hordes of enthusiastic followers who come to see their least favorite competitors get "bumped off." The atmosphere is festive, and in addition to oarsmen and jouster, each wooden boat carries musicians as well, so that the crew can sing as it goes into battle.

Q What country hosts an annual tuna-throwing contest?

A Popular in Australia, tuna throwing requires contestants to whirl a frozen tuna weighing about twenty pounds around their heads with a rope and then fling it like an Olympic hammer thrower. With $7,000 in prize money overall, the event is part of Tunarama, an annual festival held in late January in Port Lincoln, South Australia. Since 1998, the record holder has been former Olympic hammer thrower Sean Carlin, with a tuna toss of 122 feet.

Animal rights activists will be pleased to know that historically, the tuna were spoiled fish that stores refused to sell. In more recent years, rubberized tuna has replaced real tuna in the early rounds.

Q What do the winners in a cheese-rolling contest bring home?

A Would you risk life and limb for a piece of cheese? For competitors in the annual Cooper's Hill Cheese-Rolling and Wake, the answer is a resounding yes, indeed.

Just picture it: It's just before noon on the last Monday in May in western England's Brockworth, Gloucestershire, and the hills are alive with the sound of voices chanting, "Roll the cheese!"

Welcome to Cooper's Hill, which is actually more like a cliff: a 215-yard-long, almost completely vertical incline averaging a 1:2 and sometimes even 1:1 ratio in some places—a 70-degree angle nearly perpendicular to the sky. It's so steep, say locals, that the sun's rays never fall directly on the slope. So steep that it's impossible to run down and maintain balance. So steep that more than 100 people show up every year to race, tumble, and/or fall down the hill, chasing after an eight pound wheel of cheese the size of a dinner plate.

Welcome to the annual Cooper's Hill Cheese-Rolling and Wake. No one is quite sure when the tradition began, but the earliest written record of the event is  from 1826—and even then it was considered an old favorite.

Today, runners come from all over the globe to compete in one of five races, held at twenty-minute intervals.

After an arduous climb to the top, the runners—around twenty per race—sit in a line and wait for the Master of Ceremonies to escort the guest cheese-roller to his or her position. After the emcee gives the starting command, the runners scramble after the cheese, encased in corrugated paper and decorated with blue and red ribbons, which can reach speeds up to 70 mph. In rainy years, the hill is a muddy mess but easier for competitors to slide down; in dry years, the ground is a hard, unforgiving course ripe for scraping skin. To win, a runner must finish in about twelve seconds.

The grand prize, of course, is the cheese. Second and third place winners receive a small cash prize of ten and five pounds (about $15 and $7 respectively).

If it sounds ridiculously dangerous, it is. There are an average of thirty injuries each year—mostly bumps and bruises, though the occasional broken bone and concussion is not unheard of. Spectators are also at risk: Those leaning too close to the edge may fall over. Others may get hit by a runner, or by the rampant cheese.

To minimize injuries, bales of hay are perched at the bottom of the hill to catch the runners, as is a local rugby team. Also onsite is a cave rescue team, ready to climb up after fallen contestants and carry them to nearby ambulances.

Very little has ever stood in the way of Gloucestershire and its cheese roll. Even when rationing during both World Wars limited the nation's cheese supply, a wooden wheel was constructed instead, with a token nugget of cheese tucked inside for authenticity.

Recent events have also canceled the public festivities. In 1997, there was a record-breaking number of injuries (33), which led to the cancellation of the event in 1998 due to safety concerns. The roll has also been canceled because of the foot-and-mouth disease outbreak of 2001, and the unavailability of the local search-and-rescue team in 2003. But even so, the Gloucestershire cheese-rolling committee gathered together to roll a single cheese down the hill. After all, the cheese must go on.

Q Can you participate in wife-carrying if you're not married?

A You certainly can. Wife-carrying is a sport that, despite its name, is open to married couples and singles alike. Members of less-blissful matrimonial pairings might even suggest it as a way for single folks to preview the rigors of married life: Men struggle to achieve their goals while burdened by the dead weight of a clinging female; women have their world turned upside down and then are forced to kiss a man's ass repeatedly.

Sounds like fun, huh?

They thought so in Finland, where the sport of wife-carrying was invented using two colorful snippets of national folklore as inspiration. Finnish men, it is said, once chose their mates by stealing them from neighboring villages. And an outlaw named Rosvo-Ronkainen recruited his bandits by putting them through races in which they carried weighted sacks. This practice was synthesized into wife-carrying, an international competition that has held its world championships in Finland each year since 1995.

The rules are fairly straightforward: A man carries a woman who weighs at least 108 pounds through an obstacle course. (Women who weigh fewer than 108 pounds carry a sack weighted to make up the difference.) Whoever completes the 253.5-meter course in the quickest is the winner. The obstacles can include different surfaces (like sand or water) and objects (like fences).

In previous contests, men were penalized fifteen seconds each time they dropped their women. (As far as we know, the women may very well administer other penalties, but these aren't in the rules.) In the 2009 Wife Carrying World Championships, however, the fifteen-second penalty was omitted. It's not quite as barbaric as it sounds—the woman does wear a helmet, after all.

The popularity of wife-carrying has extended to other parts of the world, including the United States and Canada, other European countries, Africa, and even China. Many of the winners from these far-flung regions eventually travel to Finland to test their mettle in the world championships.

But nobody has taken to the sport quite like the Estonians. From 1997 to 2008, Estonians won eleven world titles. And one family, the Uusorgs of Tallinn, notched seven of those crowns, with Margo claiming five and his brother Madis the other two. There are a few different carrying techniques, but the crafty Estonians introduced what has become the most popular method, known as the Estonian carry: The woman clings to the man's back with her legs straddling his neck and her face buried in his posterior.

The egalitarian Finns claim that the ultimate goal of the competition is for everyone involved to have fun, but is there any doubt about whom this whole thing is really meant to benefit? The prize for the champion is his wife's weight in beer.

Q Do you have to be fat to be a sumo wrestler?

A In other words, can you be thin and compete in sumo? Not since George Carlin's comedy rant on the English language's oxymoronic couplets ("jumbo shrimp," "military intelligence") has there been a more mismatched concept than "thin" and "sumo." With good reason.

Historically, these supersize athletes (*rikishis*) have been known to dent the scales from roughly 220 pounds, which would comprise the sport's version of a 98-pound weakling, to 518 pounds. But in the world of professional sumo—with its incessant handslapping, salt-tossing, foot-stomping, bull-rushing, and chestbashing—big isn't universally or undeniably better.

In the traditional ranks of Japanese sumo, where kudos to Shinto deities to ensure healthy harvests once played as large a role as blubber-to-blubber combat, the highest order of achievers are given the honorable title *yokozuna*. (No, *yokozuna* does not translate to "Is there any more cake?")

To become a *yokozuna*, a wrestler must simultaneously satisfy both subjective and objective criteria. He must dominate in the *dohyo*, or ring, where two consecutive Grand Tournament wins are considered a nifty way to attract the eye of Japan Sumo Association judges. He also must demonstrate a combination of skill, power, dignity, and grace. Fewer than seventy men in the centuries-old sport of sumo have ascended to this lofty tier, and most have been larger-than-life figures—literally.

The twenty-seventh *yokozuna*, known as Tochigiyama, was an exception. A star of the sport between 1918 and 1925, Tochigiyama was a comparative beanpole, at about 230 pounds. Yet he proved to be a crafty tactician, frequently moving mountains...of flesh. His won-loss record was 115–8.

At the opposite end of the weighty spectrum loomed the mighty Musashimaru, the sixty-seventh *yokozuna*. He dominated the eighteen-square-foot *dohyo* while clad in his *mawashi* (not a diaper, though it looks like one) between 1999 and 2003. Musashimaru won about 75 percent of his three hundred or so bouts, due in great measure to the fearsome nature of his physique. He tipped the scales at about 520 pounds.

Somewhere in the middle, we find perhaps the greatest of them all: Taiho, who reigned in the 1960s and became the forty-eighth *yokozuna*. Taiho chalked up thirty-two tournament wins and weighed 337 pounds.

So here's the skinny on sumo wrestling: You don't have to be fat to do it.

Q Has dwarf tossing been banned in every state?

A Life was simpler back in the 1980s. It was "Morning in America again," according to President Reagan. Director John Hughes tugged at our heartstrings with movies that exposed the hardship of being sixteen, misunderstood, and rich. And dwarf tossing was in its heyday.

Indeed, the phenomenon took flight during the mid-1980s in Australia and the United States. Ostensibly a competitive endeavor, it involved an average-size person picking up a dwarf and tossing him as far as possible into some sort of landing pit, which often consisted of mattresses. Participating dwarfs made themselves more tossable by wearing padding and a harness with strategically placed handles. Cash prizes were awarded for the longest tosses.

Like loud, pointless arguments and regrettable sexual encounters, dwarf tossing appealed mainly to the inebriated, and so the competitions always took place in bars.

As dwarf tossing grew in popularity, so did the controversy surrounding it. In 1985, Chicago Mayor Harold Washington called it "degrading and mean-spirited," and the city successfully scuttled a dwarf-tossing competition by threatening to revoke the liquor license of the host bar. Other communities employed similar preventive tactics. While promoters and their fearless flying dwarfs argued for the right to earn a living, opponents cited safety concerns and the objectification of little people.

The turning point came in 1989. As the good-time 1980s prepared to give way to the politically correct 1990s, an organization called Little People of America lobbied successfully for legislation outlawing dwarf tossing in Florida. New York followed suit, and soon the dwarf toss had joined Atari, Cabbage Patch kids, and Duran Duran on the scrap heap of 1980s pop culture.

European nations issued their own prohibitions throughout the 1990s. Even the United Nations and its Human Rights Committee got involved, upholding in 2002 France's dwarf-tossing ban after it was challenged by three-foot, ten-inch Manuel Wackenheim, who said the ban kept him from earning a living.

Is it banned in every U.S. state? Hardly. Technically, it's not even banned in Florida, the Ground Zero of dwarf tossing. That was made clear in 2001 when a three-foot, two-inch radio personality named Dave "The Dwarf" Flood hired a lawyer and tried to overturn the state's anti-dwarf-tossing law.

At issue was the specific stipulation against dwarf tossing in bars. If you get the urge to fling a consenting dwarf in the Sunshine State, nobody can stop you—unless you do it in a drinking establishment, in which case the bar will lose its liquor license and be fined up to one thousand dollars.

As Flood knew, few people other than bar drunks are interested in watching dwarf tossing. Florida's law, he argued, violated his rights under the U.S. Constitution. Can you guess what happened when Flood filed his lawsuit in U.S. District Court? Yup, the judge tossed it out of court.

Can a man outrace a horse?

For an answer to that question, we could look at dry statistics of the speeds attained by various humans and horses over different lengths. Or we could turn to Wales, where they've addressed the question through rigorous experimentation.

The Man Versus Horse Marathon is an annual race between humans and horse-and-rider teams held in early June in the Welsh town of Llanwrtyd Wells. The event started in 1980 when a pub keeper overheard two men debating which was faster in a long race—man or horse. Slightly shorter than a traditional marathon, the 22-mile course is filled with many natural obstacles, and horses win nearly every year.

Finally, in 2004, Huw Lobb made history as the first runner to win the race in 2 hours, 5 minutes, and 19 seconds, beating his fastest equine competitor by about two minutes. He took the £25,000 (about $47,500) prize, which was the accumulation of 25 yearly £1,000 prizes that had not been claimed. Apparently, the horse doesn't get to keep its winnings.

In 2007, Florian Holzinger managed another win for the humans. So a person can definitely outrace a horse. That said, if you ever need to escape someone who's pursuing you on horseback—well, you might want to invest in a car instead of running shoes.

Q **Whatever happened to Ted Williams's head?**

A Where is Ted's head, anyway? It's in a barrel in Scottsdale, Arizona. To understand why the question and its absurd-sounding answer are significant, it helps to know a little about Theodore Samuel Williams.

Ted Williams was one of the greatest baseball players ever. He is to the Boston Red Sox what Babe Ruth is to the New York Yankees. Among the most feared hitters of all time, Williams is the last major league player to achieve a batting average of .400, hitting .406 in 1941. He's among a handful of players with more than 500 career home runs and was elected to the National Baseball Hall of Fame in 1966. His incredible baseball career was interrupted twice because he was a fighter pilot—yes, a fighter pilot—in World War II and the Korean War. Williams was a controversial figure, a loner who had a contentious relationship with the media. Williams was also an avid outdoorsman and, after his playing days ended in 1960, was a well-known corporate spokesman for Sears.

Anyhow, Ted's head is currently floating with several other severed heads in a barrel of liquid nitrogen at a cryonics facility in Scottsdale. His body is in another barrel, with some other optimistic cadavers.

This has been the case since "Teddy Ballgame" departed this life in 2002. It's the result of a pact that was apparently made between Williams and two of his three adult children to have their bodies cryogenically preserved. His eldest daughter challenged the validity of the pact.

Cryopreservation is the business of deep-freezing human remains shortly after death. The theory—based on various scientific principles—is that if the essential cell structure of a body is preserved, the body can be revived in the future, once the necessary technology has been developed.

Adding to the macabre specter of the "Splendid Splinter" decapitated and bobbing about in a sealed container are reports about the Arizona facility itself. A friend of Williams talked his way in and later told the media about what he regarded as unacceptable conditions, including the indignity of Ted sharing a cylinder with a bunch of average Joes. Other reports allege that some of the 182 samples of Williams's DNA that were preserved by the lab are missing.

The body of Williams's only son, John-Henry, followed Ted to the Scottsdale facility after his own death in 2004. Judging from accounts, the elder Williams was not an easy man to have as a father, and John-Henry didn't behave like a prince of a son. Here's hoping that medical science someday succeeds in reanimating those who forked over more than $100,000 to become popsicles—Ted's bill reportedly was $136,000—and that the Williams family gets along better the next time around.